STANDARD LOAN

Unless recalled by another Reader
this item may be borrowed for

FOUR WEEKS

To renew, telephone:
01243 816089 (Bishop Otter)
01243 812099 (Bognor Regis)

TEACHING PRACTICE

Teaching young children requires more than an ability to set goals, apply techniques and assess outcomes. It involves developing trusting relationships, deciding on what children need to know, creating secure and stimulating learning environments and working cooperatively with other significant adults in children's lives.

This book will help you prepare for and make the most of your teaching practice in a variety of early childhood settings which cater for children from birth to 8 years. The topics covered include ways of knowing and relating to children; the early childhood curriculum; effective social and physical environments for learning and teaching; and working collaboratively with colleagues and parents.

While giving many practical guidelines and suggestions, this book challenges you to do your own thinking about learning and teaching. It will encourage you to use your specialised and personal knowledge – to do more than 'practise' teaching techniques during your teaching practice.

Rosemary Perry is a lecturer in the School of Early Childhood at Queensland University of Technology, Brisbane, Australia.

TEACHING PRACTICE

A guide for early childhood students

Rosemary Perry

London and New York

First published in 1997
by Routledge
11 New Fetter Lane, London EC4P 4EE
Simultaneously published in the USA and Canada
by Routledge
29 West 35th Street, New York, NY 10001

Reprinted 2001 by Routledge Falmer

Routledge Falmer is an imprint of the Taylor & Francis Group

©1997 Rosemary Perry

Typeset in Garamond by
Ponting–Green Publishing Services,
Chesham, Buckinghamshire

Printed in Great Britain by
Biddles Ltd, Guildford and King's Lynn

British Library Cataloguing in Publication Data
A catalogue record for this book is available from the British Library

Library of Congress Cataloging in Publication Data
Perry, Rosemary
Teaching practice: a guide for early childhood students /
Rosemary Perry. Includes bibliographical references and index.
1. Early childhood education – Study and teaching.
2. Early childhood education – Curricula. 3. Classroom management.
4. Early childhood teachers – Training of. I. Title.
LB1139.23.P47   2997
372.21– dc21 97–473

ISBN 0–415–14882–0

To my parents,
who gave me a wonderful childhood

CONTENTS

ILLUSTRATIONS

PLATES

FIGURES

TABLES

FOREWORD

In areas of professional education and training, provision is made for students to undertake periods of practical professional experience. While this may take a variety of forms such experience has a specific objective: to assist the aspiring professional to make realistic connections between the lectures, tutorials and other on-campus experiences and the world of professional practice. In other words, such practical experience is aimed at inducting students into those realities of professional activity to which lectures and tutorials can only allude, because no matter how well prepared or delivered, they will always lack the immediacy, complexity and reality of 'real life' work.

This poses a dilemma. Short of a return to the classic model of being apprenticed to a master before acquiring 'journeyman' status, how does the student in a teacher education programme progress from student to competent beginning practitioner without succumbing to 'staff room' culture? This culture maintains the process of stasis: what has worked becomes what will continue to work. Unless student teachers are guided by motivated teachers who have a capacity to contribute to new ways of teaching – and new ways of interpreting children's responses, their progress towards becoming a competent practitioner is jeopardized.

The capacity to view teaching as a dynamic process is essential, because:

- early childhood teaching has as much to do with relations and interactions as it has to do with organization and presentation of content;
- early childhood teaching is concerned with holistic development of children as individuals and members of groups and involves attention to social-emotional development as much as to cognitive- and physical-motor development;
- early childhood teaching involves the formation of valued partnerships with colleagues, parents and the wider community;
- early childhood teaching is not bounded by the classroom but involves learning both within and away from its particular physical setting.

Katherine Read, whose textbook *The Nursery School* was used for several decades, described the early childhood classroom as a 'human relations laboratory'. While this description is too narrow and limiting because of its emphasis on the particular relations developed within a specific physical space, she was correct in identifying a unique aspect of an early childhood teacher's work: that of mediating between a range of aspects confronting children in the earliest phase of the human life span. Young children at this early stage do not make considered judgements about where they are or what connections they form. They are in a formative and vulnerable position.

Dr Rosemary Perry, whose own journey in teaching has spanned a broad spectrum of early childhood experience – teacher, advisory teacher, system administrator and university teacher – brings a unique but highly relevant perspective to bear on the matter of practical experience. She challenges the conventional view of teaching practice as the occasion where the student practitioner recreates learning acquired in lecture theatres and seminar rooms about the 'how' and 'what' of teaching young children. This challenge questions whether, in practical situations, students are engaged in 'practising teaching' or 'teaching for practice'.

While this question may appear simply semantic, the emphases have broader implications. It is one thing for a student to reproduce a set of practical techniques that have been imparted in lectures and tutorials, but it is something quite different to ask a student to think as a teacher.

Dr Perry has written from the latter perspective. In doing so she maintains an important link with earlier early childhood practitioners and creates a distance from those approaches that suggest that 'teaching is teaching is teaching'. Such a view does not form a part of an authentic early childhood approach to teaching. Rather, Dr Perry, drawing upon her own personal experiences as a teacher and her reflections as a supervisor, provides a practical and realistic set of guidelines for early childhood practice.

Professor Gerald Ashby
School of Early Childhood
Queensland University of Technology
Brisbane, Australia

November 1996

PREFACE

Purpose and content: My purpose in writing this Guide has been to assist you as a student teacher to prepare for your teaching practice experiences in early childhood settings and to make the most of the learning opportunities which they provide. In making decisions concerning the topics to be discussed I was influenced by the comments of your peers, the contributions of writers who have sought to encapsulate some of the complexities and dynamism of teaching in the early years, as well as the practical wisdom which experienced teachers have willingly shared. As a result, attention has been given to these topics – ways of knowing and relating to children; developing an understanding of the early childhood curriculum; providing effective social and physical environments for learning and teaching; working collaboratively with colleagues, parents and other significant adults in children's lives; and how to develop a practical theory and practical skills. Although these topics are discussed in separate chapters their interrelatedness is highlighted, as many underlying concepts and principles common to all topics are revisited throughout the book.

Approach to presentation: In deciding how to approach these topics I was influenced by my belief that a useful Guide talks directly to you, its reader, anticipates your experiences and questions and engages you in the learning process. Presenting the experiences of other student teachers, and, in some instances, teachers, seemed to be one authentic means of achieving such goals, as the teaching stories of others bring into focus real situations, dilemmas, issues and rewards which you are also likely to face. The challenge was to present these accounts in ways that would lead you not only to view a situation from the perspective of another student teacher, but would enable you to consider situations and behaviours in ways that fostered your own exploration of associated theories and perspectives, and encouraged you to propose possible consequences of actions as well as appropriate strategies. In short, the aim was to enable you to develop your own knowledge of the 'what' and 'how to' of teaching.

In creating this type of presentation, judgements had to be made concerning the extent and nature of the coverage given to theory, research and specialized knowledge and the amount of space allocated to personal stories. For example, it was considered important to provide you with sufficient theoretical and specialized information to build a meaningful context for the discussion of each topic as well as to extend your understandings. It was also considered, however, that the students' accounts of their experiences would provide you with relevant information of a different type. For instance, students' stories show how understandings of important concepts may develop, how ideals and goals can be transformed into practice and how effective strategies can be derived by reflecting on one's own or another teacher's practice. Because the development of both types of knowledge – the theoretical and the practical – was considered necessary, a balanced coverage of both these aspects was attempted.

Philosophy: As I wrote the book and selected stories I was aware that certain philosophical views about teaching and teacher education were influencing my decision making. These views may be summarized as follows:

- *Learning to teach is a very personal process.* Because, as a student teacher, you bring your own unique past experiences, current understandings, expectations, learning style and personality to the teaching practice setting, your experiences and learnings will differ from those of others. Teaching practice will necessarily involve you in developing awareness of your own strengths and weaknesses and in meeting personal challenges. In the process of learning to teach you will begin to make explicit the beliefs and values that are guiding your actions and decision making, and, as you reflect on your experiences and seek to derive personal meaning from them, you will find your own answers to your teaching dilemmas. No one else can do this for you.

- *Learning to teach involves recognizing the complexity of decision making.* Teachers have many different reasons for acting and responding in the way they do in particular situations. These reasons may relate to beliefs and assumptions about learning and teaching, understandings of children or situations based on specialized knowledge, obligations to meet curriculum requirements and professional responsibilities, as well as the recognition of personal skills and abilities that they can offer. In other words, as a teacher, you will have to make decisions about your actions in the light of your analysis of events, your specialized knowledge, your responsibilities and your consideration of possible consequences of alternative strategies. It is important that, as a student teacher, you come to recognize and accept the complexities inherent in teacher decision making and that there is no one 'correct' method that can always be applied. In order to deal successfully with this complex decision making you need to learn to reflect on your knowledge and actions in ways that lead you to deeper understanding of learning and teaching.

- *Learning to teach is a continuing and constructive process.* Just as children need opportunities to contribute to their own learning, take the initiative, set goals, deal with problems and gain confidence from their achievements, so, too, do you as a student teacher. You have to become an active participant in your learning to be a teacher. Although on-campus courses can provide you with theoretical knowledge about learning and teaching and provide information as to 'how to' handle particular behaviour and situations, it is only as you set yourselves goals, take the initiative and deal with problems that arise during teaching practice that this knowledge is used and a new dimension of practical knowledge constructed. Provided you critically examine and reflect upon your teaching experiences you will continue to construct 'new' knowledge throughout your years as a student teacher and then as a teacher.

Given this philosophy, the stories presented were not only selected because they gave some insight into the particular topic being discussed but also because they indicated how particular goals and strategies were derived, demonstrated ways in which reasons for the making of particular decisions could be clarified, or illustrated growth in a student's personal understanding of a teaching issue. This book could not have been written if students and teachers had not been willing to share their experiences – their successes and their moments of despair. In some stories the students were happy for their real names to be used, while in others, names were changed at the students' request. To all those who contributed I say a big thank you.

A brief background: All the student teacher contributors are from the School of Early Childhood within the Queensland University of Technology and have undertaken or are currently enrolled in a four-year Bachelor of Education degree specializing in early childhood education. This course requires them to undertake teaching practice in at least three different early childhood settings, which must include:

a long day-care setting:	providing for babies–5-year-olds for periods up to 12 hours per day and where attendance may be on a regular or an occasional basis;
a preschool setting:	providing for 3–5-year-olds in 2½ or 5-hour sessions and where attendance is on a regular basis on consecutive or alternate days;
a lower primary school setting:	providing for 5–6-year-olds (Year One), 6–7-year-olds (Year Two), and 7–8-year-olds (Year Three) who compulsorily attend for 6 hours on a daily basis.

Although there is some variation in the use of terms to describe these settings in the literature, the terms 'long day care', 'preschool', and 'Years One, Two and Three of primary school' have been used consistently throughout this book.

ACKNOWLEDGEMENTS

As in most projects such as this there are many people to thank. To those who commented on the early drafts – Sue Armstrong, Margaret Henry, Deborah Gahan and Amos Hatch I would like to say how much I appreciated their constructive criticism and supportive comments. I would also like to express my thanks to my friends and experienced practising teachers, Sue Thomas, Gay Burgess and Fay Haas, who keep me in touch with the realities of teaching young children and have provided some of the revealing anecdotes for this book. To the Queensland University of Technology, the Head of the School of Early Childhood – Professor Gerald Ashby – and to my research assistant Shanti Balda and the Centre of Applied Studies in Early Childhood, I am indebted for their practical support and encouragement, which has made the writing of this book possible. I would also like to thank Vivienne Harris and Margie Crombie for their assistance with the photography and to the centres in which the photographs were taken – the Lady Gowrie Child Centre, Northgate State preschool and primary school, and the Chapel Hill kindergarten.

Above all I wish to express my gratitude to the student teachers who have so willingly shared their stories and experiences of teaching practice and taught me so much about the process of becoming a teacher. Thank you – Bronwyn Aird, Samantha Lee Anderson, Kay Beattie, Kym Blank, Ben Campbell, Allan Davison, Melissa Deakin, Kerrylyn Doocey, Fiona Dunn, Lana Edmonds, Karen Ellis, Louise Ellrott, Danielle Frey, Susan Glass, Korina Gole, Jodie Holding, Kirsten Ivett, Lena Jensen, Lynette Kai, Luke Kelly, Cindy Keong, Fiona Langton, Tania Masci, Kylie Patterson, Sherrin Proctor, Rachell Rendall, Tammy Shaw, Tina Stannard, Melinda Taylor, Maria Thurlow, Suzanne Tomkins, Monica Treschman, Joanne Warren, Nicole Wickham, Tania Wilcox.

1

TEACHING PRACTICE IN EARLY CHILDHOOD SETTINGS

In this chapter we are thinking about:

• what teaching practice is;
• the learning opportunities which teaching practice offers;
• preparing for teaching practice.

> One day, as 4-year-old Sam sat beside his teacher, he said, 'You must have to do a lot of learning to be a preschool teacher.'
> His teacher said, 'Mmm . . . yes, you do.'
> 'You must have to watch a lot of kids' television programmes,' said Sam.
> 'Yes', said the teacher, 'that's one of the things. . . .'
> 'What else did you have to learn?' asked Sam.
> 'Well,' said his teacher, and paused, as Sam seemed about to add more of his own thoughts.
> 'You'd have to learn about making . . . and gluing . . . playing . . . doing puzzles . . . writing and reading books . . . building games . . . painting . . . talking . . . using good ideas . . . and you'd do a lot of knitting them all together,' contributed Sam.
> 'Yes', replied Sam's teacher, 'teachers learn all about those things, and we have to learn a lot about children . . . and think about what they know and do . . . and think about what we do.'

At this point, Sue, the teacher who was recounting this conversation, said it was interrupted.

From Sam's perspective it was important that teachers learn to do all the things that children enjoy. From his teacher's perspective these learnings were important too, together with gaining knowledge about children and developing an ability to reflect and act on this knowledge. Coupled together, Sam's and his teacher's ideas about what an early childhood teacher needs to learn provide a succinct overview of the contents of this book. In using this Guide to assist you in making the most of your teaching practice experiences you will be challenged:

- to build relationships with young children (by enabling children to do what they enjoy doing);
- to extend your understanding of curriculum (by thinking about how children learn and what they need to know);
- to provide supportive learning–teaching environments (by recognizing the physical and social factors that contribute to learning);
- to develop your practical theory and practical skills (by thinking about what you do, how you do it, and why);
- to collaborate with other important adults in a child's life (by refining communication skills and establishing working relationships).

In developing your knowledge and abilities in relation to each of these aspects you will also be challenged to do 'a lot of knitting them all together', to use Sam's phrase, because it is in this way that you build a more complete understanding of what it means to be a teacher of young children.

WHAT IS TEACHING PRACTICE?

Teaching practice refers to the period of time in which you, as a student teacher, gain first-hand experience in working with a particular group of children in an early childhood setting. A number of terms such as 'the practicum', 'student teaching', 'field studies', 'infield experiences' or 'internships' are used to refer to this period. In this book, the terms 'teaching practice' and 'the practicum' will be used. The one exception will be when quoting students' comments in which they make reference to their teaching practice and use the student vernacular 'prac'. Teaching practice can be undertaken in a number of forms, such as in two to four week blocks, a day per week over a term, or as an internship following the completion of a theoretical course.

During your teaching practice you are generally guided by the teacher responsible for the particular group or class to which you have been assigned. In this book, this person will be referred to as your *supervising teacher*, although elsewhere this person may be known as the 'centre-based' or 'school-based' teacher, the 'cooperating' teacher or the 'resident' teacher. When undertaking your teaching practice you also may have access to a representative from your university or college. This representative, who is likely to be responsible for advising you and for liaising with the supervising teacher, will be referred to as your *university teacher*.

TEACHING PRACTICE: BECOMING PROFESSIONAL

Teaching practice has become an integral component of most pre-service teacher education courses (Lambert, 1992; MacNaughton and Clyde, 1990; Posner, 1993; Tisher, 1987). Perhaps because it is regarded as one of the most important means of assisting students to become early childhood teachers, many have mixed feelings of anticipation and apprehension as they commence their teaching practice. Tina, for instance, after her first visit to her teaching practice centre wrote in her journal:

> After today I can say I am excited, happy and full of anticipation. Yet I am also full of fears and worries. My excitement and all the other positive feelings come from the fact that I really relate to the type of programme at the centre. It is one which helps children learn through expressing their own ideas and making their own choices about activities. This is great, but I am a little worried as I have never experienced a programme where the children have had quite so much choice and input. For the first couple of days, I hope I can spend a lot of time observing. I do believe I can learn a great deal here. I just hope the children accept me and that I'm able to become a contributing member of the centre.

Do you have the same mixed feelings about teaching practice that Tina experienced? There's the excitement of being a part of a *real* early childhood setting, of getting to know children and their families, of planning and organizing the day or of extending a child's understanding. At the same time there are the niggling doubts about your ability to cope with unfamiliar situations, manage the whole group, or establish a working relationship with your supervising teacher.

Although all of your teaching practice experiences will contribute in some way to your understanding of teaching it is important that you learn how to *use* your experiences in order to learn the most from them. Katz (1984, 1995a) has suggested that becoming an early childhood professional involves:

- developing specialized knowledge;
- using that knowledge to assess and make decisions;
- acquiring high standards of practice.

It is important that you think about how to use your teaching experiences to develop your knowledge and abilities in relation to each of these aspects.

Developing specialized knowledge

Although you can gain much specialized knowledge by attending lectures and undertaking readings and assignments during courses on campus, when you enter the teaching practice setting this knowledge can be given added meaning. As one student, Rosanna, said: 'When I came into contact with *real* children and parents, and *real* teachers and classrooms, I discovered that I became less sure about some things and learned a whole lot of new things about something I thought I knew well.' Comments made by students in

Plate 1.1 Although beginning to play with others, 2-year-olds seek the attention of adults. (Photo courtesy of Lady Gowrie Child Centre, Brisbane.)

discussions I had with them as their university teacher during a recent teaching practice indicate that this is a common experience. For instance, Danielle, a student in a day-care centre, described how her knowledge of 2-year-olds had been affirmed:

> At Uni we were told that 2-year-olds are beginning to like pretend play and I've noticed that this group just loves home corner . . . so yesterday I went in to them and they were making cups of tea . . . and I said to Jay, 'Do you think Mike would like a cup of tea? P'raps you could ask him,' and he did . . . and you should have seen the look on Mike's face. He was so pleased.

As Danielle drew on her knowledge of 2-year-olds to guide her actions and observed their effects, she was also discovering new knowledge about 2-year-olds, having never worked with that age group before. She said:

> They need a lot more reassurance about everything compared with 3-year-olds . . . like 3-year-olds are more able to play with each other while 2-year-olds are more inclined to have parallel play. The other day I did a sociogram of two little girls, Rachel and Heather . . . and it was really interesting to see how Rachel moved from one thing to another without once interacting with anyone . . . and Heather kept coming and talking to me. She wouldn't talk to other children. She'd only talk to me. So they really seem to prefer to talk to adults than children their own age . . . although I try to get them to talk to each other.

By the second week of his teaching practice with a group of 4–5-year-olds, another student, Tim, had become particularly aware of the respectful relationship between the teacher and the children. He felt this contributed to a very positive environment for learning. Tim said: 'I can see how Miss S treats children individually. She really values their contribution. . . . She doesn't come across as being superior. She never raises her voice and yet the children always respond.'

I asked Tim whether he had noticed anything in particular that Miss S did in order to create this positive atmosphere. Tim thought before he replied:

> Well, she really listens to what they say . . . and she often makes comments such as, 'That's a good idea' or 'That's good thinking'. And if she asks them to do something, she explains why it needs to be done . . . like at tidy up, they all sit down and think about the jobs that have to be done and she makes it clear what she expects them to do. They talk about what their jobs are so it's very clear, and the tidying up gets done.

Tim was aware of the children's positive attitude to learning and that the teacher was contributing to this, but he needed the question to spark further thinking about some of the specific strategies the teacher was using. Asking yourself questions about what is happening and why things are happening in certain ways is a vital part of developing your specialized knowledge during teaching practice.

Felicity, a fourth year student, was beginning to look at her specialized knowledge and ask herself questions about it in the light of her own values. During my visit we had been discussing her goals for the children and what she felt it was important for them to learn. Here are some excerpts from that conversation.

> Felicity said, 'I think it's how children get on with others ... and what they learn about themselves that's important. Sure they've got to learn subject matter and skills ... but well, I believe children have to know themselves and know how to be with other people before they can learn anything else ... because if they can't accept themselves they're not going to learn.'
>
> I asked her if that meant that the kinds of goals she would focus on would be related to children's social abilities and needs.
>
> Felicity said, 'Yes ... though I would also aim to develop abilities in other developmental areas. I think other things are important as well ... but to learn other things you've got to know about yourself. If a child is always going to be fighting and always on the outside ... that child's not going to learn anything. Do you understand what I'm saying?'
>
> I replied that I did. Then Felicity asked, 'Well, is what I'm saying right or wrong?'
>
> My immediate response was, 'There's no right or wrong answer. It's a decision you have to make in the light of your knowledge.'

Making assessments and decisions

Felicity's question – 'Is what I'm saying (or doing) right or wrong?' – highlights the dilemma that lies at the heart of every decision or judgement an early childhood teacher has to make. I've thought long and hard about whether my response to Felicity's question was the appropriate one. The more I've thought about it the more I've realized that, in teaching, there is no simple answer to this question. As Katz (1984: 3) points out, these decisions and judgements involve 'diagnosing and analysing events, weighing alternatives, and estimating the potential long-term consequences of decisions and actions based on [specialized] knowledge'. That is quite a task even for the most experienced teacher! Fortunately, pre-service courses offer you time and assistance in developing the skills which contribute to your ability to make sound professional judgements. You are not expected to make these decisions in your first teaching practice. Rather, the practice teaching situation is seen as the place in which you can develop skills that will help you make decisions. It is important, then, to clarify what these skills are so that you can begin to practise them.

The teaching cycle

In order to make teaching decisions you will need skills that enable you to:

- *Describe events*: This necessitates observing the actions of all those involved – the child, other children and adults – and recounting the situations that arise and the interactions that occur. As well, you should try to identify some of the factors that appear to contribute to the situation.
- *Reflect on and analyse situations*: This means thinking about the situation in ways which focus on *what* happened, *how* it happened and considering possible reasons for *why* it happened. In order to do this you may need to look in depth at the interactions and responses of both children and adults. If you are the adult involved it is important to be as objective as possible about what you did and why you did it, while at the same time recognizing the feelings you may have about the situation.
- *Consider alternative strategies*: Having analysed the situation you are in a better position to think about the ways in which the situation was managed and how it could have been handled differently. For instance, your analysis may have indicated that the squabbles that are happening with the 3-year-olds are likely to be due to there being only two trucks and four children who want them! In the light of your knowledge of 3-year-old development you may decide to provide more trucks for the group. Similarly, your analysis of the unruly noise emanating from your Year One class may have indicated that the children are unclear about ways to use the two new learning centres you have set up. Clearly, some rules are needed but there are differing ways you could handle this situation. Do you write down some rules and present them to the class or do you call a class meeting and involve the Year One children in making rules that have particular meaning for them?
- *Decide on and carry through a course of action*: The knowledge that you have thoughtfully analysed situations and considered alternative strategies gives you confidence to put your plans into action. These plans may involve providing particular materials or equipment, focusing a discussion, or being near a child in a particular situation to provide support. Generally, well-thought-through plans succeed. Occasionally, however, even after much consideration you may find that your chosen course of action is not working or not having the desired effect. Always be prepared to modify or change your approach in these circumstances. For this reason it is useful to have planned an alternative course of action.
- *Evaluate the effectiveness of decisions and actions*: By the time you get to

do this you will feel that you have come full circle, because, in order to evaluate, you are back to observing and describing the situation. After all your effort, it is likely that you will be able to note improvements in the situation or in the children's behaviour or knowledge. You may see improvements in the children's use of the materials, or in the quality of the interactions between children or between the children and adults. These evaluations, while in one sense being an end point, also provide you with a new starting point for further planning.

The process containing all the actions outlined here is commonly referred to as the *teaching cycle*. It is an important process to keep in mind because it highlights the various skills needed in order to make professional decisions. Louise, a beginning student teacher, used a number of these skills as she focused on her interactions with Lilly. The way in which she did this is illustrated in this extract from her teaching folder. Louise wrote:

> *Description of the situation*: Since my first day at the preschool, 5-year-old Lilly has been my shadow, following me everywhere and attempting to monopolize my time and attention. I have explained to her that I have to spend time with all the children and that while I like to play with her I can't be with her all the time. This morning I was out in the playground looking at a shady patch in the garden when Lilly joined me. Lilly said, 'This is like a beautiful rainforest garden. I wish I could hear the sound of trickling water.' I agreed with Lilly that the shade and green plants did make it seem like a rainforest and we discussed her experiences of visiting a rainforest. She talked about 'the tall trees', 'walking along tracks', 'hearing water trickle over rocks' and 'making little waterfalls'.
>
> *Reflecting on and analysing the situation*: As we talked, I realized Lilly had quite some knowledge of rainforests that I could perhaps extend. I also knew that Lilly liked a challenge and could probably work out a way to make the sound of trickling water. I also thought that this might be a project she could undertake with other children and without me.
>
> *Carrying through a course of action*: Before I was really aware that I had decided on a course of action, I said, 'How do you think you could make some trickling water?' I used lots of open-ended questions. Lilly decided she would need a pond for the water to run into, as well as some rocks for the water to run over. We began to think of the things she could use to build the pond – some plastic sheeting; spades; watering cans; and some logs and rocks. I helped Lilly collect these materials and encouraged Stephanie to join in as she showed interest in what we were doing. As we couldn't find any large rocks we used two bricks instead.
>
> When the girls began digging the hole for the pond I moved away

and observed from a distance so that the girls could direct the play. Annemarie joined them and they worked well together without conflict. When they felt the pond was big enough I helped them line it with the plastic before they placed the bricks on top of the log to form the waterfall. They then began to fill the pond by pouring water from their watering cans on to the bricks and watched it run into the pond.

I decided to use the teachable moment and talk to the children about forests, plants and ponds. I asked them, 'What creatures live in ponds?' Annemarie said that frogs and tadpoles did, and added, 'If we leave the pond here, they might come to live here.' We decided that we would leave the pond there overnight. The children continued to play in the pond, floating leaves and bark in the water. They particularly enjoyed pouring the water over their feet. I found myself reminding them to be careful not to stand on the plants that were nearby. Lilly suggested they could make paths to the pond by putting rope down so the plants wouldn't be trodden on. This proved to be successful.

Evaluating the effectiveness of decisions: The next morning I decided not to mention the pond so as to see if the children were genuinely interested. Lilly and Stephanie went to the pond immediately they entered the playground, although after a few minutes, Lilly came and grabbed my hand and asked me to come to their pond, which I did. After noting there were no tadpoles yet they began to play in the pond and added more water. Lilly did not seem to need me so I moved away and observed from a distance.

I feel that this experience was worthwhile and meaningful for all concerned. The activity related to the children's past experiences – they knew about trickling water and rainforests. Working on the pond gave the children a range of sensory experiences – smelling and feeling the water and moist earth and listening to the sound of the running water. I tried to get them to talk about these sensations to increase their awareness of them but they found this difficult. Lilly, Annemarie and Stephanie maintained a high level of attention and they explored a range of concepts such as sinking and floating; full and empty; plants, growth and forests.

Self-evaluation: I am happy with the way I guided this activity. I realize that I may not always be able to give so much attention to one small group when I am responsible for interacting with the whole group. My initial questions for getting the children to be more aware of their senses need to be improved. When I talked to my supervising teacher about this she suggested that, instead of asking, 'How does it make you feel?' I could have shared some of my thoughts – 'This trickling sound reminds me of bath time when the tap is turned on just a little.' She said she has found that such examples often help children to express their own thoughts. She also suggested posing some 'wondering' type questions – ' I wonder why the soil here feels so moist and cool?' I will read a book tomorrow about rainforests with a view to developing their concepts further.

From this extract it is apparent that Louise, in writing about the event after it had happened, used the skills that are a part of the teaching cycle as a useful framework for clarifying her thinking about the experience. Her account shows that she became aware of the learning opportunities inherent in Lilly's comment, analysed the situation and decided on a course of action almost simultaneously. She then described 'the action' and 'interactions' in some detail before seeking to evaluate the effectiveness of the experience from both the children's perspective and her own. Written in this way this account suggests that the skills outlined in the teaching cycle are used in an ordered, sequential fashion. Although this may sometimes happen, it is far more usual that two or more of these skills are being used simultaneously. One experienced teacher told me that she frequently found that in her teaching she was simultaneously using all the skills in the teaching cycle. They were 'jumbled together'.

When Melinda told me of her interactions with Owen during her recent teaching practice in a Year One classroom I was reminded of just how 'jumbled' the use of these skills can be. Melinda said:

One of the best things that has happened to me this prac is that the children have really responded to me . . . well . . . except for Owen. He just won't stand up and participate in morning talk. He seems a very bright child, and on the odd occasion when he does say something or join in, he has a great contribution to make. I've been trying to reinforce his behaviour when he does participate . . . giving him lots of praise. But then at other times he gets a look on his face . . . an 'I'm not going to do this' look. I know he can do it, but at these times he just won't, and I don't know why.

The other day we were playing 'Doggie Doggie where's my bone' and I asked who hadn't had a turn . . . and he put his hand up . . . and I chose him. I don't know why I did that because the whole day we'd been having these tussles. Anyway, after I picked him he wouldn't go and get the bone . . . so I went over to him, took his hand and took him over to the bone . . . and he picked it up . . . and I thought, 'OK we're fine now' . . . but when he got back to his place he wouldn't sit. So I stopped the game and I said it was a pity that we couldn't go on playing it because we were having to wait for Owen to sit down. But Owen kept standing there and the other children were becoming restless . . . and, I don't feel good about what I did, but I felt it was the only thing left to do . . . I said, 'OK, if you don't want to join in the game then there's no point being here' . . . and I removed him over to the corner. I felt really awful but I made him sit there while the other children worked on their ideas for the circus ... and then I went and talked to him, and I said, 'It was because you weren't participating I put you here ... I thought you didn't want to be involved in the class.' He started crying and I felt terrible. I asked him if he could tell me what the problem was but he wouldn't talk, although I knew he was listening to me. So I kept on talking ... saying how I had been sad because I knew he could join in and do all these things ... and I said a lot of positive things about him ... and I said that I couldn't understand why he wouldn't join in.... And something must have clicked ... because yesterday he did join in!

The principal came in when I was taking a group ... and I picked Owen ... and then I thought, 'Oh no, what have I done?' But he responded ... and a few other times during the day he joined in. You could see he thought hard ... but then did it. And he responded to the music teacher this morning ... and he's never done that before ... and this morning at the end of the group when I said I was going to write on the blackboard he came up to me and gave me this piece of chalk. He looked so pleased as he gave it to me ... and he said, 'You won't have to look for a piece now.' I don't know where he got the chalk from.

From listening to Melinda's description of her experiences with Owen, it was apparent that her observations had contributed to her understanding of the situation. As Melinda interacted with Owen, she was constantly reflecting on and analysing the situation as well as thinking about the strategies she could use that would encourage his participation. In the game of 'Doggie Doggie', Melinda was faced with one of those moments when immediate action is required. With Owen standing and obviously flouting the rules of the game, and with the other children becoming restless, Melinda had to decide on a course of action. She did not have the luxury of time to consider alternatives. She decided to act, and followed through on her decision to remove Owen from the group. But that wasn't the end of the situation. Later Melinda went and talked with Owen. She shared her reasons for her course of action and clearly indicated that she valued him as a person and wanted to understand Owen's reasons for his behaviour.

Melinda's evaluation was able to include some very positive outcomes for Owen and herself.

I really would have liked to find out why Owen was behaving in the way he was ... because I didn't like what I did ... although I had tried all the positive things first. But it worked ... and I'm really able to give him lots more positives now. Like yesterday when I was with him I said, 'I feel so happy to see you joining in like you have been.' He said, 'I'm just so tired I want to go home.' It really is an effort for him ... and he came to me this morning and talked to me. At the end

of this prac I'm really feeling I can teach . . . that I can problem solve.
I think my experience with Owen has really helped me to do that.

Melinda's story of her experience highlights the importance of being able to observe, describe, reflect and analyse, as well as to make decisions, use effective strategies and to evaluate. Although Melinda was using all the skills highlighted in the teaching cycle she was not using them in any set order. Rather, she was continually drawing on each of those skills and frequently using them simultaneously. They were in fact 'jumbled together'. As she acted on her decision and removed Owen from the group she was observing his reactions and those of the other children, analysing them, considering further strategies for rebuilding her relationship with Owen and continuing to manage the group. As well, she was reflecting on her own feelings about whether or not she had done the right thing. Melinda's account of her experience is a good illustration of the complexities of assessing situations and making decisions.

Acquiring high standards of practice

As a student undertaking teaching practice, you may feel that the need to adopt professional standards of practice or a code of ethics is somewhat irrelevant – something for the distant future when you gain a position and officially enter the early childhood profession. You do have responsibilities in this regard, however. Because you are undertaking teaching practice in settings where there are young children who are powerless and dependent on adults for their physical and psychological well-being, standards of professional practice become particularly important (Katz, 1995b). Although as a student teacher you may not have full responsibility for the children, there will be many occasions when you make decisions or act in ways that can have considerable impact on their lives.

Some guidelines for ethical practice for early childhood students undertaking teaching practice have been proposed by the Early Childhood Practicum Council of New South Wales (*Guidelines for Ethical Practice in Early Childhood Field Experience*, 1995). Some of the aspects highlighted by these guidelines, together with other issues associated with ethical behaviour, indicate that acquiring high standards of practice involve:

- acting in ways that best serve the interests and well-being of children;
- ensuring that confidentiality about children and their families is maintained;
- adapting and responding to the unique services and features of the setting;
- recognizing, accepting and valuing diversity among children, families, and members of staff;
- acting in accordance with the legal and industrial aspects relating to the teaching practice setting.

Plate 1.2 Young children are dependent on adults for their physical and psychological well-being. (Photo courtesy of Northgate State Preschool.)

Serving children's interests

As a student in the process of developing your professional expertise, it is not always easy to know which is the best way to act. It has been argued that the difference between professional and non-professional behaviour is that non-professional behaviour is 'determined by personal predilection, common sense or folk wisdom' while professional behaviour is influenced by special-ized knowledge and accepted principles of practice (Katz, 1984: 9).

I am sure that there will be times when you find yourself taking a common-sense approach or acting in ways in which your parents or a respected teacher treated you. This is not something to feel guilty about, but it is something you need to consider in the light of the specialized knowledge you are acquiring. It may well be that after reflection you will want to add these strategies to your professional knowledge base because you can see that they are consistent with your new knowledge or with accepted principles of practice. There may well be other strategies you decide to discard.

Maintaining confidentiality

Sometimes a supervising teacher will share confidential information with you so that a child may be better understood, or a family situation may be discussed at a staff meeting so that staff are in a better position to support the family. It is essential that you respect the personal and confidential nature of

13

this information and do not discuss it with other students, friends or parents. Even comments made to another staff member, if overheard by a parent or child, can be misinterpreted or repeated causing much heartache to those involved. When writing or discussing observations and child studies or when participating in on-campus seminars relating to teaching practice, you should take care not to use real names so that particular children, parents or staff members are not identified.

Adapting to the uniqueness of the setting

Different early childhood settings may demand very different responses from students. For example, if you are undertaking teaching practice in a long day-care centre you may be required to attend at the time of a particular shift. If you are in a classroom where parents are regular participants in classroom activities, you will need to be prepared to welcome and work with additional adults in the room. If you are undertaking teaching practice in a centre which shares its facilities with another organization, you may be asked to assist in packing materials and equipment away at the end of a session or week. It is important that you recognize and accept the unique features of your teaching practice setting and show that you can adapt to the demands they make.

Valuing diversity

Given that one of the dominant values in our society is that everyone be treated with equal respect, you must demonstrate sensitivity to a wide variety of backgrounds, family structures and individual needs and abilities. This respect and sensitivity can be shown in your own interactions with children and adults, as well as by encouraging children to develop positive attitudes towards others with different backgrounds, social customs and abilities.

Becoming familiar with legal and industrial aspects

Because laws, regulations and industrial awards vary between states and local authorities it is important that you become familiar with the particular legal and industrial requirements relating to the centre where you are undertaking teaching practice. Some issues you should enquire about relate to licensing; funding; child space and building regulations; liability and duty of care; work place, health and safety regulations; as well as the industrial conditions and awards that apply to the staff at your school or centre.

TEACHING PRACTICE: OPPORTUNITIES FOR LEARNING

In this chapter we have been considering teaching practice in terms of the opportunities it offers you to extend your specialized knowledge, to use that knowledge to assess situations and make decisions and to show that you are beginning to acquire high standards of practice. As you commence your teaching practice and struggle to get to know the children and adults, become familiar with the routines and work out what is expected of you, it may be that you feel more overwhelmed than excited by these learning opportunities. Don't be alarmed if you feel this way. Many students have similar feelings initially. Take heart from the fact that by the end of the teaching practice most students agree that they have learned a lot from the experience. Here are just a few of their positive comments.

JAY I've learned so much. I've never had a group quite like this … and I've had to use a lot of management strategies … and develop them. I've never had to do that before.

TINA I've had to learn to plan from my observations. Mrs H doesn't believe in putting out activities just because there's a space. In this Centre everything that's put out is there for a reason. So I've learned how to go about doing that.

DANIELLE I hadn't realized that working with toddlers was just so full on. You can't switch off for a second.

MELINDA I've learned that I can teach Year One children. I've really enjoyed planning a unit of work. I've loved putting my ideas to the children and seeing them work on them … and having children respond to me as if I was their teacher … and I've proved to myself that I can problem solve … and handle difficult situations.

On rare occasions, some students experience difficulties in their teaching practice and feel far from positive about their learnings. I well remember a practicum I had in a preschool in my first year as a student that left me feeling frustrated and bewildered. At the time I couldn't put into words what it was that concerned me, but, with the benefit of hindsight, I'm sure my frustrations stemmed from my supervising teacher's desire for order and tight control. I was expected to keep the children occupied doing activities set by the teacher. I could see that the activities held little enjoyment or meaning for the children and allowed them no opportunity to diverge or imagine.

I remember one day being told to sit at the sewing activity and teach the children to sew according to the teacher's set procedure. While two children were managing to remember to thread the bodkin *down* and then *up* from *underneath*, the third child, Sarah, was becoming hopelessly confused and upset. Rather than persisting with the set task, I encouraged her to make stitches as best she could and soon she had a much-stitched, scrunched-up ball of fabric and a beaming face. 'It's a new ball for Joey, our kitten,' she said as she put it in her locker.

That afternoon my supervising teacher informed me of the error of my ways with Sarah. I was told of the importance of teaching a correct procedure and of getting children to persist at a task so they could achieve. I felt a failure and yet I felt that Sarah had achieved. She had made something of which she was proud. I felt, too, that my encouragement had contributed to her achievement. Was I really such a failure? There were many similar experiences during that teaching practice. I wanted to encourage the children to play, to diverge from the set activity which seemed to be in direct opposition to what my supervising teacher wanted. Which approach was most appropriate? Was I right or wrong to think this way?

I have often thought about that teaching practice. As I became more aware of my emphasis on meaningful activity and play in my own teaching, I realized that I and my supervising teacher had experienced a very clear mismatch of values and teaching approaches. Even though at that stage my teaching approach was embryonic, I was coming to recognize that encouraging children to act on their own ideas and valuing what children perceived to be of value were important aspects of my teaching. At the time I considered that particular teaching practice had been a disaster. In retrospect, I realize that it helped me make some important discoveries about my own teaching. It also helped me define things I would not do as a teacher, although it took me some years to be able to explain why I believed they were not good strategies. So you see, even negative teaching practice experiences can result in positive learnings!

The students' comments and my own experience indicate that the learning derived from teaching practice will be different for every participant. Given that every group of children, every supervising teacher and every student teacher is different, this should come as no surprise! As you come to reflect on your own experiences in becoming a teacher you will realize that learning to teach is a very personal process. As you undertake readings, assignments and lectures, observe experienced teachers, listen to the teaching practice experiences of others as well as reflect on your own, your understanding of teaching will continue to deepen. These events will also be 'mixed together or integrated with the changing perspective' provided by your growing awareness of your own values to form your own 'practical theory' (Handal and Lauvås, 1987: 9). There is no one way to teach. Every student teacher and every teacher is continually developing a personal approach to teaching. In becoming a teacher you have to be prepared for some personal challenges.

PREPARING FOR TEACHING PRACTICE

Once your practice teaching placement has been confirmed there are a number of actions you can take that will help you feel 'prepared'. Here is a list of tasks you may wish to undertake:

- Telephone the centre or school and arrange a mutually convenient time to meet your supervising teacher.

- See if it is convenient to make a number of classroom visits to familiarize yourself with the children and the setting before your period of teaching practice officially begins. (In some courses this may be a set requirement.)
- Gather as much information as you can during these visits. Aim to get to know the children, the staff, the facilities and resources available within the setting, the nature of the programme and the administration of the school or centre.
- Accept that your supervising teacher may not be able to spend a lot of time with you during these initial visits because priority must be given to the children and parents. Be prepared to use your initiative during these visits, but remember, too, that you are still a visitor.
- Ask questions of staff members when they have time available. They will not think your questions silly but will be pleased that you are keen to find out.
- Make contact with your university teacher. Discuss any concerns and share your hopes for the teaching practice.
- Be sure that you fully understand the expectations of your institution regarding your role as a student teacher during teaching practice. If you are uncertain, discuss these expectations with your university teacher before teaching practice commences.
- As you become familiar with your particular school or centre, consider the ways in which you will be able to meet the requirements set for your teaching practice.
- Discuss these requirements with your supervising teacher and be prepared to negotiate ways of achieving these, taking into account the particular features of your teaching practice setting.
- Be prepared to seek and accept advice. Let your supervising teacher know that you are keen to learn and would appreciate any feedback.
- Think about ways in which you can share your thoughts, ideas and 'wonderings' with your supervising teacher.
- Avoid jumping to conclusions about whether the teaching you are observing is 'good' or 'bad' after only one or two visits. Be prepared to keep an open mind until you have observed and experienced the situation for a considerable length of time.
- Think about the level of your commitment to the teaching practice. Remember that you will have to allow time for written reflection and preparation, apart from the time you are with the children. Work out how you are going to handle other personal or job commitments during the teaching practice.

Being prepared for the unexpected

As you prepare to undertake teaching practice be prepared for one more thing – the unexpected! There are many circumstances, and combinations of factors, that can influence the nature of the experience. These reflections of students highlight a number of unexpected factors which they encountered.

SUSAN   I have a 2-year-old son, so I thought doing a prac with the toddler group would be easy because I felt I knew that age group . . . but I've found it difficult interacting with several toddlers at the one time. I also found myself dealing with my own emotions about putting my child in long day care when any of the toddlers became upset.

JENNY   I'm supporting myself through Uni and have this job in after-school care. It's very hard to juggle prac and my job. It makes for some very long days . . . and nights.

ROSS   I've found it very difficult coming into this primary prac. I've been in preschool and long day-care pracs before this and I've found it difficult to adjust this time. There seems to be a different form of organization here. . . . You have to stick to the timetable and the children have to go to the library and music at set times. . . . I also have to be aware of the syllabus documents when I'm writing my objectives.

These unexpected experiences challenged the students to make personal adjustments in the way they approached their teaching practice. Meredith, a rather shy student, recounted another type of difficulty that had arisen for her through lack of communication between herself and the supervising teacher. In her interim report half-way through the practicum, the supervising teacher, Toni, had commented on Meredith's lack of contact with the parents and the children in the 3-year-old group on their arrival at the centre. Meredith had a different perspective.

I thought that greeting the children and parents was Toni's job and I thought that if I went and took the children from the parents she'd think I was taking her role. I guess I should have asked what my role was . . . what she expected of me. But I didn't. I just found my way as we went along. And I find I'm still feeling a bit nervous about whether I'm doing what Toni expects me to do.

Meredith realized that she had to know far more about the expectations her supervising teacher held for her. As Toni did not spontaneously communicate these, Meredith had to work out a way of eliciting them. As well, she realized that she needed to share some of her own perspectives and concerns with Toni. In contrast, Claire, a confident, outgoing student, was presented with a very different type of challenge by her supervising teacher, Anne. As they discussed the interim report, Anne indicated that she felt Claire was demonstrating that she was a satisfactory student but that she had a lot more potential. She wanted Claire to show her that potential. Claire said: 'I've been racking my brains ever since to see what I can do to show Anne what I'm capable of. . . . I thought I might ask if I could take more responsibility . . . plan and organize a whole day.'

18

All these accounts highlight factors that resulted in some unexpected challenges for students during their teaching practice. Although you are the one who has to meet the challenges, remember that you have others who can assist you. Talk over a situation with your supervising teacher or your university teacher. Share a difficulty with a fellow student or friend. Consider their perspectives together with your own as you think through ways of meeting the various and unexpected challenges that will inevitably arise during teaching practice.

SUMMARY

Teaching practice enables you to gain first-hand experience of working with young children in early childhood settings and provides countless opportunities for developing your professional understanding and teaching skills. The extent to which you learn from these opportunities is largely up to you, and will depend upon your willingness to:

think about your practical experiences in the light of your theoretical knowledge;
practise and refine those skills that are a part of the teaching cycle;
develop an understanding of high standards in teaching and ethical practice.

Your supervising teacher and university-based teacher are there to support you in your learning, but you will need to share your aims, concerns and feelings with them if they are to assist you. There are a number of steps you can take to prepare for your teaching practice. These include familiarization visits, clarifying the requirements expected of you during the practicum, and organizing other aspects of your life so that you can give a high commitment to teaching practice.

There will be many occasions during your teaching practice when you will ask, 'Is what I'm doing or thinking right or wrong?' While your supervising teacher may help you find some solutions, it is vital that you seek to come up with answers or to make decisions that have meaning for you. Be prepared to accept that there may be no clear-cut answers or absolutely correct ways of handling particular situations. Rather, there may be a number of alternatives that need to be considered in making a decision. In seeking solutions to teaching dilemmas you will be required to do your own thinking in the light of your growing specialized knowledge and understanding of effective practices for young children. These are the challenges and rewards that teaching practice offers.

SUGGESTED ACTIVITIES

- Role play your initial visit to the centre or school where you will undertake your teaching practice. Prepare for role playing by considering the situation from the perspective of each participant (for example, the supervising teacher, student teacher, aide, children, director or principal). After the role play discuss the interactions and reactions of the participants. What are some strategies, attitudes and questions that you as a student teacher can adopt in order to make this initial visit a positive experience for all? What actions are best avoided?

- In small groups, write down what you would like to know about your teaching practice setting and how you could gather this information during visits made prior to the commencement of teaching practice. Remember to ask your supervising teacher for advice concerning your ideas before undertaking these activities.

- Discuss the teaching cycle. After viewing a video, reading a scenario or actually experiencing a situation which requires some teacher action, use the processes suggested to make some decisions. Although it may not be possible actually to carry through your course of action, outline your strategies and develop criteria you could use to evaluate their effectiveness. Share your thoughts and any difficulties you may have experienced and consider how these could be overcome.

- Discuss the standards of practice expected of students that are outlined in this chapter. Think about the practical ways in which you can demonstrate that you are acquiring high standards of practice in your particular setting.

- Read and discuss the professional code of ethics or practice that is adopted by teachers in your area. Give reasons for why you think a professional code of ethics is important.

2

WAYS OF KNOWING AND UNDERSTANDING CHILDREN

In this chapter we are thinking about how we can come to know children by:

- developing relationships with them;
- considering ways in which observation assists our understanding;
- using knowledge gained from observation to guide teaching actions.

TEACHERS AND CHILDREN: BUILDING RELATIONSHIPS

Coming to know children and building relationships with them are two of the most exciting yet demanding challenges you will face as a teacher. If you are to enable children to engage in meaningful learning experiences and to approach learning with confidence it is vital that you and the children know each other well and build mutually trusting relationships. In order to develop this knowledge and construct these relationships both you and the children will need to find out how the other thinks and feels, what each can do, and how each is likely to behave in particular situations. Although it is to be expected that as the teacher you will have a far more detailed knowledge of children than children will have of you, and that you will show far more empathy and unconditional positive regard than the children, it is important to remember that coming to know another person and building an effective relationship requires the contribution of both parties.

It also takes time to achieve these goals. Trusting relationships are generally built as children and teachers talk and join together in play and other activities, as well as observe each other in everyday situations. If the duration of your teaching practice is only a few weeks, the challenges of building trusting relationships are even greater. You will be surprised, however, at the amount of knowledge you can gain in a short period of time, and at the strength of the relationships that can develop if you really set out to 'come to know' children. In developing relationships you should be prepared to accept that you may not always be 100 per cent successful. Leanne's account of her experience during a recent teaching practicum provides a reminder that success in establishing relationships is not always assured despite your best efforts. Leanne wrote:

Forming relationships with children is something I have always taken for granted. It is easy to do, isn't it? Well, before my last prac I thought it was. Until then, this had been the case for me. At my last prac, there was a child who displayed quite a lot of negative behaviour. I believe in being positive, so I aimed to focus on positive aspects. Unfortunately, I did not ever have detailed conversations with him, although I tried. He answered my questions and then would ask me to leave him alone. I do not think he disliked me, nor do I feel I spent my time harassing him. It seemed more that I was a stranger, an intruder, someone who was interrupting him. I simply wanted to get to know Larry as much as I wanted to get to know all of the children and their perspectives. Larry stood out in the group. He was not afraid of defying anyone, or of being different. I was concerned that I was not getting to know him.

One day I did a transition activity with the children to get them to wash their hands before morning tea. Larry refused to move. My mind raced with strategies I could use to persuade him to join the others. I knew telling him to do it was not going to work. I sat at his level and said his name, loudly enough to gain his attention, yet in a way that I thought would avoid a confrontation. Before I had finished he turned his back to me and shouted, 'SHUT UP'. The teacher came over and told him it was time to get ready for morning tea and he joined the other children. I had not even uttered a sentence.

It hit me right then. I had no relationship with Larry. I had tried . . . but I had only been at the centre two weeks. This was my first real taste of not getting to know a child as well as I would have liked. The teacher told me she still struggles with Larry and she has been with him all year. I got to know almost all of the children at my prac, yet when I left I still didn't know Larry. They say, 'Out of sight, out of mind'. Well Larry may be out of my sight but he certainly is not out of my mind. Larry taught me that forming relationships can be a challenging task, more challenging than I had ever imagined!

As you set about getting to know children and building relationships with them, you may find it useful to recall Leanne's experience. Although you will be able to build positive relationships with most children, don't be too hard on yourself if you find relationships have not flourished to the extent you had hoped. Remember, developing trusting relationships takes time and effort from both parties.

Some suggestions for getting to know children

Here are some ideas and experiences of other students which may help you think about how you can use your time most effectively in coming to know the children in your teaching practice setting.

Become familiar with names and faces

If you have the opportunity to visit the centre a number of times prior to commencing your teaching practice, you should be able to write down the first names of children from the class roll and begin to link some names with faces as you observe the children in their play or class activities. Coming to know children, however, means far more than getting to know their names and faces, or even observing them from a distance.

Talk with the children

In my experience, observing from a distance provides a different form of knowing someone from that experienced when you are able to talk with a person directly. For instance, getting to talk with someone at a party whom you had only previously observed across the room, provides you with opportunities to check out your initial impressions. Being able to interact with young children as they play provides you with similar opportunities. It also offers the child a chance to get to know you. In your visits prior to the teaching practice, ask your supervising teacher if you can talk with the children and join in class activities.

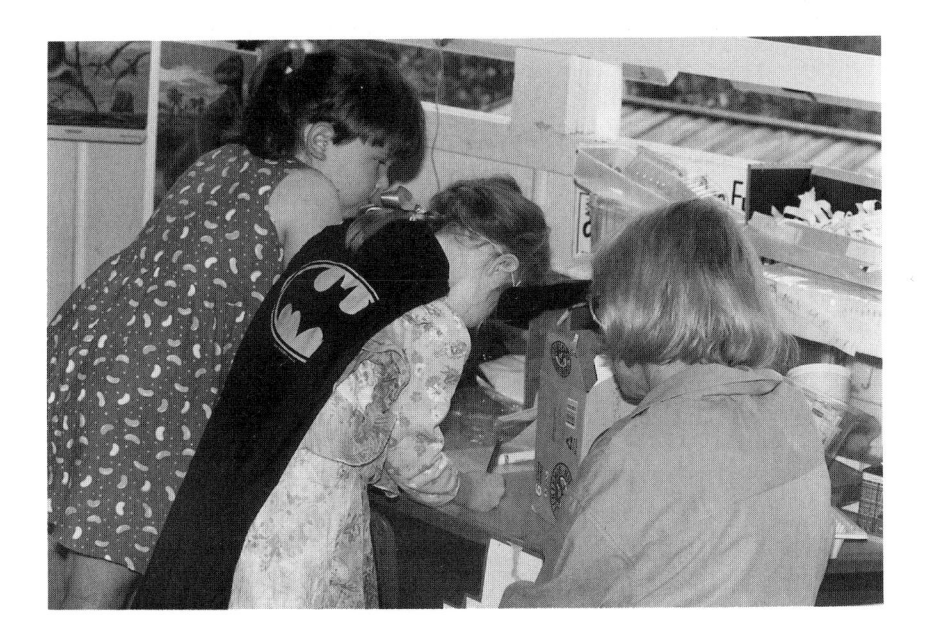

Plate 2.1 In getting to know children it is important to show them you are interested in what they are doing. (Photo courtesy of Northgate State Preschool.)

Think about how children might see you

Are you this tall person who towers over them, or are you someone who squats or sits down with them as you talk? Are you another child's mother or father who is visiting? (How many times have I been asked, 'Are you Jay's mum ... or grandma?'!) Do you explain who you are and why you are there? If you ask a child their name do you tell them yours too? That seems only fair. Do the children see you as someone who is watching them or as someone who is interested in what they are doing and might join in their game?

Join in activities with the children

Jenny, a student I visited recently, had discovered that it wasn't as easy to join in the children's games as she thought it would be. She described her experiences this way:

> Well ... there was this group of children ... and they weren't in any particular area so I approached them ... but they just looked at me when I tried to talk to them ... so throughout the day I made a deliberate effort to go and talk to them individually. They were mostly role playing, so I'd go up and ask if I could join in with them ... and later during the day ... they seemed much more comfortable and they began approaching me. If they're uncomfortable with you ... they just won't talk to you.
>
> My supervising teacher told me that a good way to join in the children's role play is to take on an 'as if' role ... so ... if they are playing hospitals I could act 'as if' I'm a nurse ... or a mother with a sick baby. I saw the teacher doing that the other day. She dabbed some red paint on the doll's arm ... and ... she went into the hospital ... and she said, 'Doctor, could you look at my baby. She's hurt her arm.' The doctors and nurses responded like it was real.... I was amazed.... They bandaged the doll ... and one wrote out a prescription and told the teacher she had to take it to the bank! I don't feel very confident about doing that sort of thing ... but I'll give it a go.

As Jenny found, you have to make a deliberate effort to join with children in play. Taking on a role in keeping with the game, or contributing some additional materials that the children can use, are useful ways to enter the play. Such actions also give the children 'cues' that you are a player too!

Share something of yourself

Several students have told me that they have found it useful to introduce themselves to the children by telling the children something about themselves.

24

Anne showed the children a photo of herself at their age. The class was particularly interested in family photos at the time. Marie found herself telling a group of children who were discussing how hot they felt that she had been so hot the previous afternoon she had gone to a friend's house and plopped in her swimming pool. To her surprise she had seen a water dragon on the side of the pool watching her. The children were immediately fascinated by the water dragon and wanted to know what it looked like, so Marie promised to bring a book which had a picture of the water dragon. As soon as Marie arrived the next day, Jason asked her if she had brought the book. Marie felt that this mutual interest helped her establish rapport.

Keep a journal

Although not a requirement, Bronwyn kept a journal of her thoughts and experiences during the days she visited the centre prior to commencing her teaching practice because she felt it helped the familiarization process. Although her journal covers many aspects of the centre's functioning, such as the organization of the day and what the teacher and aide did, only extracts which focus on getting to know the children are included here.

Monday, 25 July
I found the children's 'show and tell' to be mostly 'tell', which was great. Sarah spoke about riding on a ghost *train* which triggered a memory in Joe about visiting the place where his mum had formerly lived and was now a ghost *town*. During outdoor play I had little opportunity to observe the teacher as I became caught up in the croquet. I was unsure whether to let the children use the equipment in their own way or show them the usual way. I did suggest an easier way to some, but after a few putts they reverted to swinging the mallets like golf clubs. Later the teacher demonstrated the usual croquet position to the group.

Monday, 1 August
The day's programme began with a group discussion. Emma had a self-made folder of drawings to show. Dean had a postcard of Puffin' Billy. Dominic brought a book about space and showed the page with a picture of a dish for receiving satellite images. This led to talk about the reception of sound waves by our ears. The group discussion concluded with the children talking about their ideas for indoor time. Emma made a house. When I visited, she was cutting up brown paper to make chocolates to put in a chocolate box.
Dean made his Puffin' Billy from blocks and cushions, and some stop and go traffic signs. Gary, after discussing Puffin' Billy with Dean, decided to make Thomas the Tank Engine and used the large hollow

block into which he fitted two chairs. Patrick set up a bowling alley with Edward. They kept a score sheet. Dominic constructed a space message-receiving station from blocks and an umbrella. Sarah built a jewellery shop from blocks and gathered some jewellery. Melissa, Belinda, Katherine and Jalyce were ballerinas and stuck numbers on the chairs in their theatre.

One aspect I find fascinating is the amount of discussion which takes place. The detailed plans for what and where, with whom and with what equipment the children will work must surely help prevent conflict. Negotiations concerning positions of buildings and equipment take place publicly, so that other children are able to help the parties involved come to an agreement. This also must build a sense of community as they find out how they can pursue their interests without infringing the rights of others.

A comment on problem solving. . . . When an argument brewed with Dean's group re the action to take at the amber light . . . slow down or wait . . . the teacher advised the children to watch what their parents did when they were driving. She did not give her opinion as to the right and only option.

Monday, 8 August

The children appear to need to dress up before they begin their play, although the outfits do not necessarily reflect their roles. While the children are beginning to accept my presence and request my help with physical needs, I feel I have not become a 'playmate' as yet. For example, when I requested an appointment at the hairdressers, Emma said she was busy with her family. Later at group time she must have remembered this incident, and said, 'You can come tomorrow.' As my imagination can carry me away I must be careful to follow their lead and not take over or direct their play.

While I cannot generalize from only three mornings with the group, I am interested that each time the children with ideas for games seem to be Sarah, Emma, Andrew, Patrick, Gary and Joshua . . . or, at least, these are the vocal ones. It will be a challenge to see whether this bears out research that we discussed in class that there are dramatists, explorers (builders) and spectators. I look at Melissa and Belinda and wonder what is going on inside their heads. They seem too quiet. (Gary thinks Melissa is wonderful!)

Monday, 15 August

Gary occupied a great deal of the teacher's time today as she sat explaining the consequences of his behaviour to him and giving him the social phrases which will help him make friends. Many of the children must struggle to see another's point of view. Their own desires close their vision. The support they are being given while they learn these skills is really warm in this centre. An example of this scaffolding was when Gary announced, 'Melissa, I'm gonna sit near you.' Melissa refused and Gary reacted angrily. The teacher explained to Gary that if he were to get a mat for Melissa and put it near his mat he could say, 'Melissa, you can sit beside me, here.'

My observations of the children, whether written or just in mental note form, still tend to be in the 'getting to know you' style. My goal is to be able to focus on the children's strengths and needs so that planning for the extending or challenging of the children as individuals can take place.

In her journal Bronwyn was making some interesting 'getting to know you' type observations. It is worthwhile examining these in more detail as they provide some insights into the nature of observation as well as suggesting ways in which initial observations can be focused effectively.

THE NATURE OF OBSERVATION

Have you thought about what it is you are doing when you are observing children? Some experienced teachers, when discussing this question, described it in these terms (Perry, 1989: 2):

ANNE   When I'm observing I'm trying to build a picture of a child.

JANE   For me, observation is more than building a picture of a child. It's more than looking at what a child is doing. I have to act on the observation in some way ... try to understand what I'm seeing ... make some sense of it.

SARA   When I'm observing I think I gather snippets of all types of behaviour that help me come to know the 'Tim-ness of Tim!' I want to know all those things that make Tim, Tim ... that demonstrate his uniqueness. Things like the way Tim does things, the way he approaches other children or adults, the complexity of his dealings.

If we look more closely at Bronwyn's observations made in her journal, we can see a number of the features of observation highlighted by these experienced teachers. For example, Bronwyn was actively involved in her observations, gathering snippets of information about individual children in order to build a more complete picture of them and making connections between this new information and her previous readings and knowledge. Although each of us has to work out our own ways of observing and building relationships, it is useful to consider and try out some of the methods and processes that others have found helpful. Here are some of the processes that were a part of Bronwyn's initial observations.

Processes that are a part of initial observations

Identifying characteristics of individual children

Bronwyn did this by noting what particular children were interested in doing; what they liked to talk about; how they went about doing things; what their particular needs seemed to be; and how they got on with other children and adults.

Noting general characteristics of children

For Bronwyn these general characteristics included the ways in which one child's expression of thoughts triggered another child's thinking (for example, talk of ghost trains led to talk of ghost towns); the apparent need for children to dress up before they commenced their play; and how hard it is for some children to see another's point of view. She also noted that some children are very vocal and able to express their ideas while others are very quiet and reveal little of their thoughts.

Describing how the group functions

The amount of discussion and negotiation concerning what, where, with whom and how ideas and games would develop surprised Bronwyn, but led her to ponder on their value in preventing conflict and the sense of community they seemed to engender. Similarly, the warm support, scaffolding and modelling of phrases by the teacher with Gary was considered likely to foster more social behaviour.

Assessing how the children respond to you

Bronwyn found that she had to earn the children's acceptance in their play and that this took time. Being prepared to accept Emma's initial negative response to exclude her from the hairdressers was important, as was being aware that she must not take over the children's play by imposing her own ideas when Emma eventually invited her into her game.

Considering new information in the light of specialized knowledge

Although it is not easy to consider your observations in the light of your specialized knowledge, it is important that you try to do this. In some courses students are asked to focus on particular aspects of child development or learning and teaching during teaching practice. This was the case for Bronwyn. She had chosen to focus on two teaching issues: helping children to resolve conflict, and helping children to become confident problem solvers. By reading articles on these topics prior to teaching practice she was aware of some of the issues involved and so was able to focus some of her observations from the outset. The readings also provided her with some specialized knowedge against which she could consider her own observations and experiences.

Having a purpose for your observations

In getting to know children, Bronwyn's aim was to discover 'their strengths and needs' so she could plan in ways that challenged and extended them. Although discovering children's strengths, needs and interests are useful starting points for your planning, you will need to go on to find out far more about each child if your teaching and the children's learning is to be meaningful and purposeful. In fact, getting to know children is a never-ending process. On the last day of your teaching practice you should be discovering something new about the children.

WHAT CAN BE OBSERVED WHEN GETTING TO KNOW CHILDREN?

Because there are countless numbers of things that could be observed in getting to know children it is often difficult to make decisions about what you will observe. Here are some aspects that experienced teachers indicate they aim to observe in getting to know children:

- areas of development (e.g., physical, cognitive, social, emotional, moral);
- the children's knowledge;
- the particular skills and strategies used in learning and interacting;
- the children's dispositions;
- the children's feelings;
- the dynamics of a group of children.

These aspects may provide a framework for your observations too. The brief discussion of each of these aspects which follows may also assist you to make meaningful observations.

Areas of development

Knowledge of child development provides you with an understanding of the changes in children's thinking, feeling and behaviour as they grow from birth to adulthood, and with an awareness of the general characteristics likely to be shown by children in their various stages of development (Sebastian-Nickell and Milne, 1992). Although children are whole beings and you want to come to know them in a holistic way, sometimes it is necessary to think

29

about particular areas of development to get a more in-depth understanding of an individual child.

If you know what is involved in social and emotional development, for example, then you will be able to observe these areas of a child's development in a meaningful way. Because Moira, a student teacher, was aware that strong attachments to parents are an important base for a young child's ability gradually to establish bonds with adults and peers outside the family (Berger, 1991; Sroufe, 1985), she was able to recognize the significance of 3-year-old Rae's continual questioning, ' Is my Mummy coming now?' during her teaching practice. Similarly, when Rae ran to hug Moira before she departed with her Mum, this observation was seen as a significant step in Rae's developing ability to establish relationships with other adults. Having some knowledge of this area of child development Moira was able to bring some specialized information into her thinking about Rae and ask some relevant questions:

> Is Rae's behaviour typical for her age? What situations are likely to be difficult for Rae? Is it important to be close by when Mum is departing and to work on developing my relationship with Rae? Would a more predictable daily routine help Rae establish when her Mum will come?

From Moira's example you can see that knowledge of areas of development provides information that helps you formulate numerous questions and think about how you can respond to children in ways that assist their learning. Numerous texts on child development (such as Allen and Marotz, 1989; Beaty, 1990; Berger, 1991; Berk, 1994; Rathus, 1988; Sroufe, Cooper and De Hart, 1992) provide detailed discussions of the various developmental areas. You are strongly urged to become familiar with such texts, if you have not already done so, in order to extend your specialized knowledge of child development. These texts can provide you with some pointers concerning what to observe in specific areas of development. As well, your knowledge of development may help you understand better what you have observed. This was Anne's experience. She wrote:

> I couldn't understand why Caitlin, a 5-year-old in a Year One class, was having such difficulty doing the task I had set. Groups of children had been asked to look through magazines and cut out pictures of items for their particular shop. We were making big posters displaying what was sold by various traders such as the butcher, baker, hardware merchant, jeweller and fruiterer. Caitlin was in the butcher's shop group, but, instead of cutting out items for the butcher's shop, she cut out pictures of things that she liked and wanted. At the end of the time she had pictures of dolls, diamond rings, a bicycle, nail polish and ice-creams. Although she could tell me that butchers sold meat and recognized pictures of chops and sausages, she seemed unable to cut out pictures of meat which obviously didn't interest her. As I observed

Caitlin's behaviour, I realized that here was an example of pre-op-erational thinking in which Caitlin's egocentrism was preventing her from breaking out of that particular mind set. This knowledge of development helped me accept Caitlin's behaviour and lessened my frustration. I realized she wasn't being naughty. She just could not see why she needed to cut out pictures of meat when there were so many interesting pictures of things she wanted to have.

The children's knowledge

Although children's knowledge is frequently talked about, there are various views as to the nature of that knowledge. Some writers (Edwards and Knight, 1994: 39) argue that knowledge means not only facts 'but also skills and procedures, as well as a system of interrelated concepts'. Others, such as Katz (1996: 138), suggest that young children's knowledge can be thought of more broadly in terms of 'understandings, constructions, concepts, information, facts, stories, songs, legends and the like'. Much debate revolves around the actual content of these understandings or concepts, and what needs to be taught in order to achieve the knowledge and skills a community considers it necessary for adults in their society to have.

For those of you undertaking teaching practice in settings where children have reached the compulsory school age, observing children's knowledge may not seem to be such an issue, because with the introduction of national curricula in many countries, the *what* of children's learning is generally specified in subject-orientated curriculum documents. You may see observing children's knowledge in these settings as just a matter of observing whether or not children know the content that is prescribed. Leaving aside the thorny question of how best to assess this knowledge, there are many other questions and issues, however, relating to children's knowledge that you need to consider. Does the focus on prescribed content provide a sufficient base for the understanding of children's knowledge? Is prescribed knowledge the only knowledge that is important to young children? Are there different types of knowledge? (for example, is knowing how to climb a ladder a different type of knowledge from knowing how to count to ten?) Is the way in which children construct their knowledge important? And what about the know-ledge of children who are below the compulsory school age? What is the nature of their knowledge?

Perhaps this observation shared with me by a teaching colleague, Sue, will help you think further about some of these questions and the nature of young children's knowledge.

Sue, the teacher, was walking past a group of 5-year-old girls chatting together. She heard Cecelia comment, as she flipped her long blond hair back over her shoulder, 'If you don't have long hair when you go to school, the boys won't love you.'

Sue paused and interposed, 'Oh I don't think that's right.... I've got short hair and I know lots of people love me ... and Bridget, you've got short hair ... do you have people who love you?'

Bridget said thoughtfully, 'Yes, Cecelia! People love me....'

Sue continued, 'Yes ... and it's not what you look like or whether you've got long hair or not. People love you if you're kind and think nice things inside.... But they don't like you if you're unkind and do unkind things.'

The teacher left the group at this stage, but later in the session Cecelia came up to her and said, 'Miss T ... I'm unkind, but my Daddy says he loves me.'

Sue responded with a question, 'Oh, are you really unkind? What things do you do that are unkind?'

Cecelia replied, 'I kick people ... and sometimes I lie on the floor and scream if I can't get what I want.'

Sue replied, 'Well ... Mummies and Daddies like yours are really special people and they love you no matter what you do.'

'Mmm,' said Cecelia, thinking hard.

'But, you know', said the teacher, 'not everyone is like your Mummy and Daddy. Most people, if they see someone doing unkind things feel sad and upset ... and they think "I don't want to be friends with someone like that!" ... and often people who do unkind things end up feeling very sad and lonely.'

'Mmmm,' said Cecelia again as she walked away.

What can be learned about young children's knowledge from this observation? Cecelia spontaneously shared her knowledge with her friends. She seemed confident about the understandings she'd constructed, and, without the teacher's intervention, she and her friends could well have gone on holding this view. The teacher, however, challenged Cecelia's statement by presenting some evidence that contradicted it, and invited Bridget to present some opposing evidence too. Having set up this dissonance, the teacher went on to provide some further information for Cecelia to think about. In essence, this was that it's not what you look like that counts but rather what you do. Sue's observation of Cecelia's knowledge could well have ended here but it didn't. The fact that Cecelia came back to the teacher in the way she did, shows how children keep on trying to make connections between what they know and new information they are given. In this instance, just as the teacher had done, Cecelia had some contradictory information to present – 'I'm unkind, but my Daddy says he loves me.' It is interesting to note how the teacher responded in this situation. She accepted Cecelia's evidence but then added more information for Cecelia to take into account as she went on constructing her own understandings.

For me, this example illustrates the nature of young children's knowledge.

It reveals some of Cecelia's understandings and concepts, as well as something of the way in which she goes about constructing these by testing ideas and considering new information. It also highlights an aspect of the teacher's role in extending – or in this case, challenging – children's knowledge. Although the knowledge that the teacher sought to build – 'that being kind is what counts' – was not specifically prescribed content, it was in keeping with the teacher's goals for the children to value and respect everyone. The teacher's initial observation, which very much involved *hearing* what Cecelia was saying, was the catalyst for the learning episode. The teacher acted on her observation by providing additional information and evidence which played such an important role in helping Cecelia construct new knowledge.

While it is important to observe and monitor children's knowledge in relation to goals or prescribed content, it is equally important to observe the children's understandings, concepts and constructions which may be revealed in their discussions and interactions, as well as in their activities and play. Such observations not only provide insights into what children know and how they go about making sense of their world, they also offer teachers important cues for extending and challenging children's knowledge.

Skills and strategies used in learning and interacting

Skills are usually thought of as actions that indicate some mastery. Because they are actions, they are generally easily observed. Strategies, too, are actions but are used with a particular purpose in mind. Sometimes they are more difficult to observe and have to be inferred from behaviour.

It is important that you observe skills related to all areas of a child's development. These include verbal and communication skills, social skills, thinking, reasoning and problem-solving skills, as well as skills associated with creating, constructing and expressing ideas. Skills inherent in the development of literacy and numeracy should also be observed. Many students have indicated that when they first start making observations, they find they focus mainly on physical skills, because these seem 'more obvious'. While observing the 'more obvious' may be a good starting point, remember that your observations should help you come to know more about a child. If you have several observations showing that a child has established hand dominance, then there is little point collecting further observations that give you similar information. Aim to observe other skills that will provide you with different or additional information.

Also, when you are observing skills, try to connect that knowledge with other information you have about the child. As one of her observations, Jan had written: 'In their physical education class Troy was able to throw the ball with his right hand and catch the ball with both hands.' When I asked her about the significance of this observation, she said: 'I'm really not sure. We're supposed to get all these observations during prac . . . so when I have a

33

spare moment . . . like when the phys ed teacher was taking the class . . .
I just wrote anything I could.'

Although this is not a good rationale for making observations, it is,
nevertheless one that is used when students feel pressured to fulfil the practice
teaching requirements. As you become more skilled in observation, however,
and experience how observations can assist you in your work with children,
your purpose for making observations will change. In Jan's case, as we talked
about Troy, she realized that she had noticed that he was having difficulty
with his writing but had not observed him closely enough to know the reasons
for these problems. She decided that she needed to observe more closely the
ways in which he went about his writing tasks in the classroom. She also
realized the importance of making connections between the snippets of
information she had about Troy if she was to assist him in his learning.

It is often after observing a child's actions or experiencing the effects of a
child's behaviour that you become aware of particular strategies that are being
employed. Have you had a child engage you in conversation or present a
persuasive argument to keep you with them, especially when they sense you
are about to leave? My 4-year-old niece, with whom I was 'surfing',
persuasively argued that I shouldn't leave the water, 'because the waves
haven't finished yet. There are plenty more waves to come!' Kirsten,
undertaking teaching practice with a Year Two class, became aware of James's
strategy when she was taking a maths lesson. She wrote in her journal:

> I noticed that James seemed to rely on Sam and Nicholas to help him
> with his maths sheet and to explain the directions to him. He was sitting
> with them initially, and when I asked him to move to his own desk he
> was reluctant and took several minutes to do so. Then he kept turning
> around and asking Sam and Nicholas what to do.

Kirsten reflected on her observation this way:

> While I think it is important that children support one another, I think
> children should know that they cannot expect their peers to do or
> explain everything for them. This seemed to be the strategy James was
> using. Encourage James to do things for himself and build his self-
> esteem. Explain that he can ask group members for help but that he
> needs to have a go himself.

Observing and being aware of the strategies children are using are essential if
your own strategies are to be effective in assisting their learning and
development.

Children's dispositions

'Disposition' is a term that is increasingly being used in the early childhood
literature. Dispositions can be thought of as 'habits of mind . . . not mindless

habits ... with motivational and affective qualities' (Katz, 1996: 138). Behaviours such as curiosity, cooperativeness or quarrelsomeness can be regarded as dispositions, as can a desire to learn, or to make friends. You can generally observe children's dispositions in the way they go about doing things. It is important to come to know children's dispositions so that you can foster the worthwhile and positive ones.

Another anecdote from my teaching colleague, Sue, provides a delightful example of 4-year-old Jack's disposition to conjecture. This was only one of Jack's many 'hopes and wonderings' expressed during his short time at the centre.

> It was in the first week of term and Jack was being helped to become familiar with the arrival routine. The aide was standing near the basket where children were placing their lunch boxes. The teacher observed that Jack seemed concerned about placing his lunch box in with all the rest, and heard him say to the aide, 'How will I know it's mine?' The aide replied that they would be able to find his lunch because his Mum had written Jack's name on it. Somewhat reassured Jack went off to play, but later in the morning the teacher was aware that Jack seemed a little troubled. On talking with him she discovered that Jack was still thinking about how he would find his lunch. 'I sure hope my Mum wrote my name on the crusts, 'cos I eat the soft part,' Jack said.

By observing Jack's initial and continuing concern, the teacher enabled Jack to express his thoughts and support his disposition to conjecture. In the process she gained a fascinating insight into his 'wonderings' about the way his Mum would write his name on his lunch. It was also an important reminder that young children's views of the world are very different from those of adults.

Children's feelings

The importance of engendering positive feelings in children about their competence, their sense of belonging and their ability to learn and solve problems cannot be over-emphasized. Failure to observe a situation closely and respond sensitively to it can often result in children experiencing less than positive feelings. Nicole describes a situation she experienced on her last teaching practice which made her aware of the need to handle situations sensitively. She wrote:

> Anna, a 4-year-old, wet herself at morning tea while sitting at the table. Miss D took her outside to the lockers to get changed while the aide cleaned up. Miss D told Anna to take off her shirt and skirt as they were wet and to put on the other dress that was in her locker. Miss D then went back inside. Later, I discovered that Anna had taken off her shirt

and put the dress on over the wet skirt. Following up on Miss D's instructions I told her to go and take her skirt off. She went to her locker to do this but didn't re-emerge so I went to see what was happening. There was Anna standing beside her locker crying because she couldn't undo the button on her skirt.

Once I realized Anna couldn't undo her button I felt so guilty. Why hadn't I asked her why she had left her skirt on? Why had I acted in an irritated way? Why wasn't I thinking? Basically I think I was just following the tone of the other staff, irritated that Anna had wet herself at such an inconvenient time and place. This is no excuse. No wonder Anna didn't feel she could approach anyone when she found she couldn't get her button undone. In fact, she did the only logical thing she felt she could do – put on her dress over her skirt.

I realized I had not been sensitive to Anna's feelings. I had not observed and thought about the situation closely. Why would she keep on a wet skirt when she could have a clean, dry dress? I thought about how intimidating teachers as authority figures could be. I want the atmosphere in my classroom to be encouraging so that children are not afraid to ask for help, or give suggestions. I learned a lot from this incident . . . that I need to put myself in children's shoes more often and think about how they are feeling and why they are behaving in certain ways.

Nicole's experience reminds us of the importance of looking at situations not just from an adult's perspective but from a child's point of view, particularly a child who may be feeling embarrassed, shy and vulnerable. Although we may not be able to observe some feelings directly, we can become sensitive to behaviour that reflects feelings.

The dynamics of a group of children

Although there is much emphasis given to observing individual children in early childhood education, it is important to remember that these individuals are also members of a group. Jane, an experienced teacher in the discussion group (Perry, 1989: 9), describes her thoughts about individuals and groups this way:

My centre is not a place where twenty-five children roam about independently. We are a social setting where personalities, ideas, characteristics and emotions merge to form the dynamics of the group . . . and sometimes the dynamite! This is the setting in which each individual operates, so it is important for me to observe the group so that I can place my growing knowledge of the individual in context.

It is also important for me to come to know the group as it develops certain characteristics over the year so that I can make predictions about reactions to teaching strategies. If I can be aware of what stimulates, satisfies or calms I am more likely to aid the learning in the play. If I can be aware of what is likely to occur when different individuals and personalities merge, I can be more productive as a teacher. As the year progresses, the whole class or some friendship groups can develop patterns of behaviour. It may be that these group characteristics are productive and positive or they may be negative ones that I need to redirect in order to promote growth.

Jane's reflections highlight the importance of coming to know the group dynamics as well as considering observations of individual children in the context of the group. As you come to know which children are likely to dominate, lead or be passive participants in group situations you are able to plan your teaching strategies more effectively.

In thinking about observing individual children's development, know-ledge, skills and dispositions as well as their group behaviours, you have probably thought of many other aspects you could observe that would help you come to know children. Observing the nature of children's play, or the ways in which they interact with materials, or engage in mathematical thinking, for example, also can provide valuable information.

As you develop your observation skills and come to know your children you will find it easier to make decisions about what to observe. Jane, an experienced teacher, when describing her understanding of observation indicated how knowing a child helped her focus her observations. She said:

> For me observation is an active process in which I am internalizing a new awareness of a child which in turn changes my perceptions or behaviours. It is a conscious thought process which interacts with what I knew in the past, what I am doing in the present and influences how I will react in the future. For instance, I might observe that Tom is crying. Because I know that Tom does not usually cry, my observation seems to focus on why Tom is crying. My initial observation that Tom is crying is only a starting point and therefore not productive in itself. For me, the observation becomes productive when I search for why and make decisions about what I will do.
>
> (Perry, 1989: 4)

Jane's experience suggests that when you 'know' children you become more attuned to 'different' behaviours, comments or reactions which create a new awareness that prompts you to observe that particular aspect more closely. For Jane, observation became useful when it increased her understanding of the child and assisted her to make curriculum decisions.

HOW ARE OBSERVATIONS OF CHILDREN USEFUL TO TEACHERS?

As your experience in teaching increases, the usefulness of observations will

Plate 2.2 A casual observation might suggest a child painting a box – a detailed become more apparent. Because you know something about children's observation revealed that a boat was being made. The challenge of observation is to gather detailed information without being intrusive. How do you obtain detailed observations?
(Photo courtesy of Lady Gowrie Child Centre, Brisbane.)

become more apparent. Because you know something about children's interests, particular areas of development, or their dispositions and feelings you are in a far better position to make appropriate curriculum decisions and develop teaching strategies. For instance, observations can be used in curriculum decision making to:

• provide supportive and responsive learning environments;
• understand specific behaviour problems;
• monitor children's progress and ascertain their strengths and needs.

Using observations – to provide supportive learning environments

If you are to teach effectively it is vital that you *use* the knowledge you have gained about children from your observations when you plan learning experiences for them. Although this use may seem obvious, you may discover, as Susan did, that it is easy to overlook the knowledge you have gained from your observations. Susan, a beginning student, shared with me one chaotic experience she had with a 2–3-year-old group because she did not use the knowledge gained from her observations when planning. She said:

Because Christmas was coming up, we were talking about what presents the children could make for their parents. I'd seen this idea for hand prints made from plaster of Paris in a book ... so we decided we'd do that. I didn't test it out beforehand ... which I should have ... and we couldn't get the plaster the right consistency and I spent ages trying. This meant the children were becoming upset and restless ... and then we couldn't have them crowding around, which they all wanted to do. When they did get a turn, they really couldn't manage it by themselves and I had to put their hand in the plaster ... and some didn't like that and cried.... And then I'd forgotten they wouldn't be able to wash their hands by themselves and I didn't have a bucket of water nearby for them to wash their hands ... and everything got splattered with plaster. It was just chaos!

In reflecting on it later, Susan realized that she had not drawn on her knowledge of the children at all in planning the activity. She had been so enthused with the hand-print idea that she hadn't stopped to consider whether 2-year-olds had the physical skills to handle the activity. Nor had she thought about the extent to which they would be able to participate or whether the activity would hold any meaning for them. She said:

If only I'd thought about it .... I've observed how messy 2-year-olds are with the paints. They just don't have the fine motor skills that this activity needed ... and I've observed that they can't wait for any length of time, and yet I kept them waiting. I know that while we're encouraging them to be more independent they still need help washing their hands ... and I should have thought how I was going to manage that part of it. I just went ahead because the hand prints sounded like a fun thing to do.... I just didn't think about whether the children could handle it.

Susan's experience shows how essential it is to use the knowledge derived from observations if you are to provide supportive learning environments. This knowledge not only helps you decide whether or not the experience you are planning is appropriate, but it can also help you to think through ways of organizing the environment so that children can participate fully in the activity, and be as independent as possible while being safe.

Using observation – to understand behaviour problems

If a child is demonstrating difficult behaviour, focused observations may help identify factors that trigger particular behaviours as well as conditions that help the child control or improve the behaviour. Lena, a final year student, noted a number of factors that could have been the cause of Andrea's behaviour. For instance, the aide of whom Andrea was particularly fond left the centre; she began complaining of stomach pains; and the home corner where Andrea loved to play became a hospital as the result of some other children's particular interests. Although at the start of the practicum Andrea was happy to play in the hospital, this behaviour changed. Lena wrote:

> By the end of my first week Andrea refused to play in the hospital. She cried and refused to even walk near the area when she went to the bathroom. She also began hiding her face and sticking her fingers in her ears at story time when hospital stories were read. The crying for Mum increased at times when she didn't like the activities offered, was expected to follow a routine, or took offence at other children's actions.
>
> Originally I thought this behaviour might have been due to the changes in the room, including having a prac student take on the teacher's role, and followed my supervising teacher's suggestions to be firm and insist she behave appropriately. This seemed to make the problem worse. As our concerns increased, the teacher and I spoke with Mum, who was also worried, and took her to the doctor. Andrea did receive medical treatment and at the same time I changed my strategies to simply accepting her feelings and concerns. I kept reassuring her that she could settle down and feel better, and that she did not have to play in the hospital. I also tried to plan activities that I thought would interest her. Whether it was using different strategies, a change in her general health or simply becoming accustomed to hospital play, I don't know, but on the last day of prac Andrea was again playing in the hospital 'fixing Jo's head by injecting it with medicine' and happily joining in the other activities.

Although Lena felt there were probably multiple causes for Andrea's behaviour which stemmed from coping with a number of changes and feeling unwell, it was Lena's thoughtful observations and reflections which led to her successful teaching strategies.

Using observation – to monitor children's progress

Although observations can help you to become familiar with children's development in different areas, if the period of teaching practice is short, it is difficult to gain a sense of the rate and pattern of children's growth and development which occurs over the longer term. Similarly, it takes numerous observations of individual children in a variety of settings, engaging in a range of activities and interactions made over a period of time, for a teacher to build a realistic and holistic picture of a child.

Your supervising teacher may be willing to share with you some of the documentation of the progress of individual children gathered over the year. In some schools each child could have a portfolio which could contain dated observations, anecdotes, check-lists and samples of children's work. By examining this documentation you can become more aware of developmental patterns and the comprehensive information that can be gathered over a longer time period. This detailed information enables teachers to assess progress and problems in a systematic way, as well as to prepare profiles or written summaries of a child's capabilities constructed from integrating information from a variety of observations and sources. Ask your supervising teacher how these individual profiles are used in your particular setting. Some teachers use them as a basis for discussing a child's progress with parents and to provide information to other colleagues working with the child. Such profiles may also assist teachers in their planning and help them be more aware of aspects of learning and development that they need to observe and plan for in more depth.

It is important that as you develop your own skills in observation you also become aware of the challenges teachers are facing in documenting children's progress. With the introduction of national curricula and the specification of learning outcomes, teachers are being asked to be more accountable, and a greater emphasis is being placed on children's achievements in relation to these outcomes. Much debate has ensued concerning how these outcomes should be measured, with some educators promoting the notion of standardized tests and developmental inventories even for preschool and Year One children. Advocates of early childhood education have strongly argued that any form of standardized testing is inappropriate for children in the early years of schooling, given the uneven nature of young children's learning and development and lack of reliable instruments (Blenkin and Kelly, 1992; McAfee and Leong, 1994). This stand has placed pressure on early childhood teachers to demonstrate alternative ways of assessing young children that are appropriate to their stage of development, while providing the information that is required in terms of accountability. As a result, the nature and value of observation is under scrutiny.

Bredekamp and Rosegrant (1992, 1995) provide some valuable guidelines for the appropriate assessment of young children. These guidelines indicate that assessment should be made regularly, in a range of situations, over time; that it should cover all areas of development and learning; that it should occur in natural classroom situations and rely on 'real' activities, not contrived test situations; that it should use a range of methods, including systematic observations, recording of conversations with children and adults, as well as collections of children's work samples; that it should support, not threaten, children's self-esteem and their relationship with their parents by highlighting what children have achieved; and foster a sense of self-evaluation.

Because it is likely that you will face accountability demands when you become a teacher, it is important that, as well as focusing on your immediate teaching practice concerns, you find out about the challenges that relate to accountability and assessment and think about ways in which these challenges

41

can best be met. If, along with many others, you are convinced of the inappropriateness of standardized testing for young children, then you will need to understand alternative forms of assessment and how they can be used to provide comprehensive information on a child's progress. You will need to consider whether observation has a valid role in assessment and how it can be used most effectively.

SOME QUESTIONS ABOUT OBSERVATIONS

As you gain experience in observing, it is natural that you will have some concerns and questions about it. Be prepared to express these and seek advice. It is only in this way that you will develop your skills as well as clarify your beliefs concerning the value of observation. Here are some questions about observation that students have raised when I have visited them during their teaching practice.

Is it OK to observe some children more than others?

In discussing her teaching, Felicity commented that she seemed to focus her attention on the noisier children and spent her time with them so they did not disturb the rest of the group. In talking over this comment, Felicity went on to say that her focus on the noisy ones worried her: 'When I go to write up my observations I sit there and I see the name, David ... and I think ... I didn't even notice him today ... and I think ... it's ones like him I should be giving my attention to ... not the ones who demand it.'

Felicity's observations, or, in this case, the lack of them, highlighted her concerns regarding her responsibilities to all the children in the group. Felicity was voicing a dilemma experienced by all teachers, not just student teachers. How does a teacher share her time and attention appropriately with all children? Felicity said that her supervising teacher had told her that if a child or group of children had a problem or particular need, then you had to spend time with them, but that she felt 'things evened themselves out over the year'. Although somewhat reassured by her teacher's comments, Felicity still felt uncomfortable and anxious about not knowing her 'quiet' children, so we talked through some practical strategies that could be tried. These included ideas for getting the aide to work with the attention-seeking children so that Felicity was free to interact with and observe the quieter children.

I also told Felicity about how Tina, another final year student experiencing a similar difficulty, was attempting to ensure that she didn't become so involved with a particular group that she was unable to move around and see every child in the time available. To increase her knowledge and awareness of every child Tina set herself the task of filling in a daily observation record in which she noted something she had observed about each child. Here is an extract from Tina's record:

Table 2.1 Extract from Tina's observation record

Child	Observation
Alicia	Music with Mrs H. Wanted to sing me a song she learned at ballet with Hannah. Really enjoys music and movement.
Sara	Made blotting paper – wanted to keep Rosie there – 'Are you going to do another one?' Really enjoyed the experience. Talked well with other children at the table.
Michael	At collage table by himself. Made a mask with Adam. Did dance for the class.
Christopher	Mother on roster. Really enthusiastic about paper making. Helped Thomas and Richard do theirs. Explained the steps.
Lucinda	Enjoyed making blotting paper. Becomes really excited – hands go everywhere. Very independent – will not be bossed around e.g., by Philip.
Rosanna	Seemed fairly quiet. Enjoyed the blotting paper activity.
Philip R	Not interested with paper activity – wandered off after a few minutes. Just seemed to flutter around – watched while other children did activities, then wandered off. Played on swings with Christopher.

After reading Tina's brief observations, those of you who are familiar with a variety of observation methods may be saying that they are not proper anecdotal records. Tina herself said that to me when she explained her notes. She said:

> I know more detailed anecdotes give me more information about a child (and I write those up separately) . . . but I find the brief daily notes more useful because they make me think about what each child has actually been doing and what they are interested in. They give me ideas for the next day. . . . That's where my planning really comes from. There seem to be so many things we could do . . . the children have so many ideas . . . but I guess that is because, on this prac, I seem to be observing all the time. I found it really hard observing this way at first, because in trying to see what everyone was doing I felt I wasn't really committing myself to anyone's play . . . but I think I've developed the knack of joining in with the children . . . and being aware of everyone else.

Tina's comments indicate that she has reached a stage where her observations have become a part of her interactions. This is the nature of observation for most experienced teachers. As Sara, an experienced teacher, said: 'I don't think I decide "now I am observing". It goes on all the time . . . while I am interacting I am mentally recording (or jotting down) and reflecting at the same time.' Tina's method of observation is certainly a very practical one, particularly if your purpose is to know something of each child's interests, abilities and needs.

What methods of observation should I use?

Are we expected to do running records and anecdotal records and all the other observation methods we've been told about? I find it very difficult to walk around with a notebook. I found the first couple of days I could, but now I want to get in with the children, rather than stand there with a pad and pencil and write things down.

This was Tracey's question when I visited her. In a previous teaching practice Tracey had been required to gather certain types of observations such as anecdotes, running records or event samples in order to develop her skill in using these particular methods. In her current teaching practice there was no such requirement, and Tracey was faced with having to decide on a method of observation as well as how to observe while she was teaching. In talking further about her concerns Tracey realized that her decision about the type of method of observation to use had to be made after asking some questions: 'What type of information is wanted?' 'How will the information be used?' 'Why is the information needed?'

She decided that if she wanted to build her knowledge of individual children then she would use anecdotal records, which are short, narrative summaries of directly observed, significant incidents. On the other hand, if she wanted to find out about children's writing skills and social skills then she would use a check-list in combination with anecdotal observations. She decided to use check-lists because she knew good check-lists contain clearly defined items that would help her quickly assess whether a child had specific skills or characteristics. She felt, too, that these check-lists could help build her knowledge about the skills necessary for writing or building social relationships, which in turn would assist her to develop more focused and responsive teaching strategies. After thinking it through, Tracey realized that the type of information required and the reasons for its collection must guide her selection of the observational method.

Tracey also came to accept that the practical realities of the classroom must influence her choice of method. Because her group was particularly demanding, she realized that it would not be possible to write detailed running records or to use a method which necessitated observing from a distance unless another adult was available to intervene if a child's physical or psychological well-being was endangered. She recognized the need to discuss her choice of method with her supervising teacher in order to see whether it was feasible in the circumstances. Tracey also saw that she needed to become more skilful at making 'jottings' that would remind her of observations that could be written up in detail later.

If you are not familiar with the variety of methods which can be used to observe and study children, there are many excellent texts available to inform you (for example, Almy and Genishi, 1979; Beaty, 1990; Genishi, 1992; McAfee and Leong, 1994; Mindes *et al.*, 1996; and Nicolson and Shipstead, 1994).

To be 'real' observations, do they have to be written down?

Fiona had gained the impression that observations had to be recorded, thought about and then acted upon at some later stage. In undertaking her teaching practice in the toddler group she frequently found herself immediately responding to what she saw happening, and wondered whether by doing this she was making 'real' observations. She told me about her experiences with Brad (18 months), who had only been at the centre a few weeks. Fiona said:

> All the time he's been here, he's done no activities, and I really wanted him to join in ... and then this morning, he was sitting on my lap watching Sam do a painting at the table ... and I thought if he had a brush he might paint too. So I gave him one and he started painting with a paint brush ... and everyone said, 'Oh my gosh ... look what Brad's doing'.... And then later he was upset and he was sitting on my lap again ... and some of the children started dancing to the music ... and I saw him becoming interested ... so I slipped him off my lap and he began to join in ... and that was good.
>
> I guess I was observing all the time. I think I thought, 'Hurry and give him a paint brush because he can lose interest quickly' ... and then I thought ... 'Well, he's really absorbed in this.... I might see if he can stand by himself and do it.' And he did ... and I moved away a little, although I was still close enough for him to see me. It wasn't that I'd planned for Brad to paint ... it just happened ... but it seemed worthwhile and I guess my goals for Brad were that he would start to join in.

I reassured Fiona that this was a very legitimate form of observation and teaching even though she had not written down her observation and planning before she acted. It involved her in linking her previous knowledge of Brad with her observation that Brad seemed interested in painting, and working out ways in which she might respond to him in the present and the future. These responses were guided by her goals for Brad which had been developed from her previous observations of him.

On this occasion she wrote her observation of Brad's 'joining in' achievements in the observation section of her teaching practice folder and reflected on her own actions in her daily journal because she wanted to consider other ways of creating opportunities for Brad to join in. Writing down your observations of children helps you deepen your understanding and refine your teaching strategies. In some instances, however, this can only be done after the event.

How do I know if my observations are accurate?

During my visit with John, he said: 'Sometimes I get really bothered when I'm writing my observations. I keep asking myself, "Am I right about this child? Are my observations accurate?" My observations must be influenced by my own biases, beliefs and feelings.'

This is a common concern among students and experienced teachers. Some try to allay their concerns by testing out the information or by checking their observations against another person's observations. Others like to observe when there is verbal interaction between the children or when they can talk with a child, as this not only gives them clues to the children's thinking, but also provides opportunities to test some of their interpretations on the spot.

Almy and Genishi (1979: 8) provide some useful guidelines and examples that may help you to ensure that your observations are as accurate and as objective as possible. They suggest:

- *Look for valid evidence.* If you are studying a child's reading ability, for instance, observe the child in a variety of reading situations using a variety of methods (e.g., anecdotal records, check-lists, conversations about the child's perceptions of the problem). Almy and Genishi point out that at one level, facts that the child seems a well-liked class member, is rarely absent, and has a father and mother who are divorced do not in themselves provide information about the child's reading ability. If, however, it has been established from relevant observations that the child does have difficulty in reading, then, at another level, the facts outlined may become valid because they provide information about the child's home experiences that may be contributing to the reading difficulty.
- *Look for valid and reliable evidence.* Almy and Genishi stress the import-ance of being tentative about information drawn from a single observation or situation. They urge caution until you have seen the information 'confirmed often enough to be regarded as typical'.
- *Look for valid, reliable and sufficient evidence.* Although emotional upset is often related to reading problems, Almy and Genishi suggest that it would be wrong to conclude that the reading difficulties resulted from the child being upset due to parental divorce. It would be necessary to check out and eliminate other possible factors such as problems with vision or

hearing, or the teaching methods being used, before any such conclusion could be drawn.

While it is important to make every effort to ensure that your observations are as objective as possible, Almy and Genishi (1979: 37) maintain that our 'emotional responses colour what we see and hear and we cannot eliminate their effect'. Rather, we have to take them into account when evaluating the evidence gained from observation. Anne, one of the experienced teachers in the discussion group, had come to a similar conclusion. She said:

> I remember getting worried about my observations being subjective. I began questioning their accuracy ... and then I asked myself why I was so bothered. They are my observations. It's my understanding of them that I have to use as a teacher. When I'm observing ... *I'm the one who is changing*
>
> (Perry, 1989: 3)

Anne's statement, drawn from her own wealth of experience, highlights what observation has to offer in both a professional and personal sense. Through observation we not only come to know and understand children, we also become more aware of our own feelings and understandings. In using observation to assist children in their learning and development, we are also using observation to promote growth and change in ourselves.

SUMMARY

Coming to know and understand children is one of the most challenging yet rewarding experiences you can have. In this chapter a number of suggestions have been made, based on the experiences of other students, which will help you get to know children and build relationships with them. It is important to remember that developing a relationship is a two-way process, and you must be prepared to accept that you will not always achieve the desired relationship with every child, particularly if your teaching practice period is short.

Talking with and observing children are key elements in developing relationships. As you gain experience you are urged to ask yourself:

- what can I observe about children?
- how can I use my observations of children in my teaching?
- how can I observe most effectively?

The discussions based around each of these questions in this chapter only begin to scratch the surface, and it is anticipated that in finding some of your own answers to these questions many more questions will be sparked. For instance, in thinking further about how you use the knowledge derived from your observations you will be faced with questions concerning whether observation can be used to assess learning outcomes, and if so, how. If you are like most other students you will also have queries as to your methods and uses of observation. Share your concerns and 'wonderings' with your supervising teacher and seek advice. Remember that the more you come to know children, the better will be your relationship with them and the more successful you will be in your teaching practice.

SUGGESTED ACTIVITIES

- Recall some of your own experiences in establishing a relationship with a child. In groups of two or three, recount how you built one particular relationship. Try to identify the factors that contributed to its development. List some skills that you feel you have which help you build relationships with children as well as other skills you may need to develop.

- Having read the views and concerns of both experienced and student teachers relating to observation, think about your own experiences. Jot down any issues and share some of the difficulties you may be having with a friend. Remember that it is important to be honest with yourself, to ask questions and to seek advice and support. (As a class you might want to compile a list of issues relating to observation which could form the basis of a seminar prior to the commencement of teaching practice.)

- Share with other students some practical ideas relating to observation (for example: how to recall significant incidents and write up detailed observations after the event; effective documentation systems you have used or seen; strategies for observing and interacting simultaneously).

- Write down your observations of a situation in which you have interacted with a child. Then put yourself in the child's place and write an observation of that situation from the child's perspective. Try to see 'the world', which may include you, the teacher, other children and the situation, through the child's eyes. Discuss these observations with another student teacher and compare the different perspectives. Is it useful to look at the situation from a child's perspective? In what ways could a consideration of the child's perspective assist your teaching?

- If you are feeling overwhelmed by all the possible aspects you could observe, discuss with your tutor the option of focusing on one or two particular areas during your teaching practice. For instance, you may wish to focus on an area of development, an aspect of knowledge, children's dispositions or the way in which the group functions. Undertake some reading on the topic before commencing your teaching practice, and, at its conclusion, outline the insights and knowledge you have gained from doing this.

• Arrange a time to talk with your supervising teacher or another experienced teacher about the emphasis on accountability and assessment. Prepare some questions in advance. Try to ascertain how these trends are viewed and what changes (if any) are being made to their teaching, documentation and other assessment procedures. Share your findings with others in a class discussion, with a view to establishing a broad picture of how current trends are impacting on the work of early childhood teachers in your area. Think about the implications of the findings for your own work as a teacher.

3

EARLY CHILDHOOD CURRICULUM

In this chapter the nature of an early childhood curriculum will be explored by:

- considering its many aspects and meanings;
- thinking about the factors that influence it;
- examining views about the learner and the learning–teaching process;
- looking at ways in which curriculum ideals can be turned into reality.

MANY DIFFERENT MEANINGS

I've lost count of the number of students, who, when reviewing their teacher education course, recall that the word that most filled them with confusion was 'curriculum'. James gave these reasons for his confusion. He wrote:

> Well, before my first lecture on curriculum I thought, 'That's easy. That's just what you've got to teach.' Was I in for a shock! At the first lecture the lecturer brought in a large cardboard box. She asked us what the box could be. People said, 'a car', 'a dishwasher', 'a television set' . . . . I wondered what she was getting at. It's all rather obvious now – curriculum can be different things to different people. I think that's what makes it so confusing. There are just so many ways you can think about it.

Another final year student, Suzanne, graphically described her encounters with curriculum in her student teacher story which she titled *A Brutally Honest Account!*

> I vividly remember the first year of my teacher education course. This one certain word seemed to evoke fear among us all. Yes, we're talking . . . CURRICULUM. I recall writing my first assignment on curriculum from a multi-cultural perspective, but not understanding at all what I had written. Over the three years my thinking about curriculum has developed, but it took until this year to confront the fearful creature called curriculum and attack it with a vengeance.

My primary school practicum in first year was my initial encounter with the beast. I struggled with acknowledging the content areas and searched the syllabus documents for some meaning. Curriculum at this time meant: Language at 9 a.m.; Maths from 9.30 to 10.30 a.m.; Morning Tea; Science 11 a.m.; followed by Social Studies at 12 noon, and after lunch (on a Friday of course), Art. It seemed so easy. All the curriculum areas were in single blocks, left out by themselves like wheelie bins in a dark street. But where were the children in all this? Did they need to be considered or was teaching about getting ideas from the 'ready to teach from' source books? This was my initial fight – the beast was too structured for me to tackle, and I needed to tame it. . . . But how? Curriculum (the beast) didn't even exist in preschool settings, did it?

I was to encounter this beast again and again in the next two years. These encounters were always gut-wrenching adventures but in my third year primary practicum we found some common ground. Hello – why were the children singing in Maths? At last, the beast and I had made friends! I found this experience uplifting. Suddenly some creative thought was being used. I was able to prepare, as my supervising teacher did, experiences which were of interest to the children and addressed their needs. Incidental learning experiences were used to extend children's learning and the children were excited about their learning. Music took a part in Science and Drama took a part in Social Studies. The curriculum seemed to flow throughout the total programme for the combined Year One/Two class. The timetable was out the window and I couldn't actually categorize one subject area as being by itself. It all seemed to make more sense to me. The fog had cleared. I had begun to look at curriculum as everything that happens in the classroom.

Suzanne's vivid account of her curriculum encounters highlights some of the complexities associated with the notion of curriculum. Some of these complexities arise because, as James's lecturer illustrated, 'curriculum' is a word that is used to mean different things.

In Suzanne's initial encounter, she was seeing curriculum in terms of the subject matter or *content* of the children's learning and the set timetable. In her third year encounter, she recognized that the curriculum was focused on the children, with the children's interests and needs being addressed and extended by the teacher. The *processes* of learning had an important place in this curriculum together with the *content*. The subject matter was integrated (not separated like wheelie bins) and interwoven with the children's interests so that learning was meaningful and relevant. Suzanne and her supervising teacher were able to match their *intentions* for the children with the children's own intentions and interests. In this sense, *intentions* were a part of the curriculum. At the end of her course Suzanne was coming to see curriculum in Connelly and Clandinin's (1988) terms as everything that is experienced in the classroom situation. In other words, she was seeing curriculum in terms of the *reality* of the classroom.

All these terms – '*content*', '*processes*', '*intentions*', and '*classroom reality*' – can be legitimately used when discussing the curriculum (Smith and Lovat, 1991). You will hear teachers talking about curriculum in many different ways – in terms of what they teach, or how they teach, or why they want children to learn certain things. Rather than feeling frustrated that there is no simple definition of curriculum, we have to remind ourselves that curriculum is a dynamic concept like 'love' or 'happiness' and means different things to different people. The next time you begin to feel confused when someone is talking about curriculum, ask yourself, 'Now what aspect of the curriculum is being talked about here?' Thinking about the many different aspects of curriculum can help you understand more of its multi-dimensional nature.

EMBEDDED IN A SET OF BELIEFS

Suzanne's reflections on her first encounter with curriculum indicate a negative reaction to the nature of the curriculum she saw being implemented. The separateness of subject areas, the inflexible timetable and the focus on content without taking into account the children's abilities and interests evoked a view of the curriculum as being 'too structured for me to tackle'. On the other hand, in her third year teaching practice, she found herself responding positively as children's interests were extended, subject areas integrated and the socio-emotional as well as the intellectual aspects of children's development were taken into account.

Have you found yourself responding positively or negatively to different curriculum experiences? Often it is difficult to express why we react or feel the way we do in different situations. Even when we can say what we like and don't like about a particular curriculum it is hard to go that one step further and give reasons for our likes and dislikes. This is because our responses are generally in line with our underlying beliefs and values. Although these beliefs and values can influence our thinking we often remain unaware of their influence.

It was only after Kay reflected on her negative reaction to one of her teaching practice experiences in a Year Two class that she was able to clarify a value she held. She wrote:

> I was told the topics to be covered, and when I was going to teach them before I even started my teaching practice. My first lesson was to cover the features of Australia – rivers, bays, islands and mountains. This introductory lesson, as I saw it, was to draw on the children's prior knowledge and build from there. When I outlined my plans I was told, in no uncertain terms, that this was a waste of the children's time and mine. I was reminded of the topic to be taught and told that what

52

children already knew was irrelevant. I bit my tongue and tried to do the job expected of me. I was to pass on the information and the children were to learn it. I found the whole experience frustrating, impossible and very demeaning. I gained something from this prac though. I now know how I will never teach.

In reflecting further on her experience Kay wrote:

I believe that I valued the children's backgrounds, interests and attitudes, far more than their teacher did. I am not saying that she was wrong . . . just that I am different.

As Suzanne and Kay discovered, their supervising teachers' actions seemed to follow from their views about the learner, the learning process and the nature of teaching. Their own reactions also stemmed from their underlying beliefs and values. It was their experiences in the teaching practice situation that stimulated them to clarify further their own beliefs. It is important, then, that in thinking about curriculum you consider your beliefs about learning and teaching. For instance, you need to think about the questions that Suzanne and Kay faced:

- Is it important for teachers to find out what children know in order to build on that knowledge?
- Should the child be an active contributor to the learning process?
- What is the teacher's role in promoting learning?
- Are first-hand experiences important in young children's learning?

As you read the literature relating to learning and teaching as well as child development, and as you undertake teaching practice, you should seek to find your own answers to these important curriculum questions. In finding your own answers you will also make your beliefs and values about learning and teaching more explicit.

WHAT IS AND WHAT SHOULD BE

After reading this far some of you are probably saying that, while in a theoretical way you can understand that curriculum has many different meanings and that it can be influenced by personal beliefs and values, you still don't understand what a curriculum *is*. Don't be down-hearted! Many students feel this way. Toni found it very difficult to come to terms with the notion of curriculum. She wrote:

Even after several pracs, the whole concept of curriculum puzzled me. I could think about it in terms of theory knowledge but I couldn't blend that theory with what I saw happening in the classroom. In my second year prac I began to realize just how complex teaching could be. Planning the curriculum wasn't just putting out activities, writing a few

53

sentences as objectives and taking a few observations of children. It had to be much more interconnected, with objectives and activities linked to observations. I left that prac with a little more knowledge about curriculum but with no confidence in my abilities to plan. Coming to understand what you're supposed to be doing is hard enough ... actually doing it is harder still!

As a practical starting point for your thinking it may be useful to think of curriculum as a plan for learning – a plan that has to be created and put into action. James, in developing his understanding of curriculum, came to realize that decision making is an important part of creating that plan. He wrote:

My first major breakthrough in understanding curriculum was the realization that it involves decision making. Although decisions about curriculum are made at a political level and at a school level, the teacher can still make some decisions at the classroom level. I got quite excited by the enormous challenge of curriculum when I read Eisner's (1985) notion that curriculum development is about changing your ideal image of education into a programme that makes that ideal a reality. That was a challenge I wanted to take up.

In thinking about how he was to meet that challenge, James said he came to see that some of his decision making would involve setting goals and objectives, and organizing the room and equipment in ways that would help the children to learn. As he made these decisions and acted upon them, he also became aware that he was making decisions in keeping with particular ideals he had for his teaching – for instance, offering children opportunities to make choices in their activities.

It is important that as you start thinking about what a curriculum is, you are also seeking to clarify what an ideal curriculum should be. Even though curriculum content may be prescribed, as a teacher, you will not only be responsible for presenting content but also for transforming your vision of all the aspects of curriculum into reality. In doing so, you will need to be mindful of the views of parents and the wider society concerning what curriculum should be. There are two important questions that can guide your thinking about early childhood curriculum. These are:

- What is it that young children should learn?
- What are the most effective ways of helping young children to learn?

My guess is that, as you undertake teaching practice in different settings, and come to understand some of the influences impacting on the lives of families, children and teachers, you will find that your answers to these questions will change and be extended. As well, as you consider our rapidly changing world and the type of knowledge and competence children of today will need in a tomorrow we can scarcely comprehend, these questions become more difficult to answer. This is yet another reason why the notion of curriculum can seem confusing – but also interesting and challenging!

FACTORS INFLUENCING EARLY CHILDHOOD CURRICULUM

In recent years there have been many changes in society and developments in other areas of education that are having an influence on early childhood curriculum. While it is important that you are aware of these trends and understand the reasons for their influence on curriculum, it is even more important that you develop ways of dealing with classroom situations that are arising from the effects of these changes. Some of these recent developments will be discussed briefly, together with some of the classroom realities that are resulting from them.

Growing diversity

The decade of the 1990s is a time of rapid social and technological change with families and children experiencing changes in lifestyles, family structures and work conditions. Attitudes and expectations are altering and reflect this growing diversity. With an increasingly multi-cultural society there is a far

Plate 3.1 Curriculum decision making involves taking into account the diverse range of backgrounds and experiences of children. (Photo courtesy of Northgate State Preschool.)

greater recognition and acceptance of diversity between cultures. Social justice issues, too, are receiving greater consideration. As a consequence, children with physical impairments are being integrated into mainstream classrooms, more attention is being given to gender issues, and support is being provided for bilingual, multi-cultural and disadvantaged school programmes. A major impact of these changes in society is that there is an increasing number of children with a diverse range of backgrounds and experiences in early childhood settings.

Being aware of these trends and understanding and supporting the curriculum changes that are occurring as a consequence is relatively easy. Facing the challenges and demands of meeting the diverse needs of these children at a practical level is not so easy. If, in your teaching practice situations, you have worked with children from different cultures, who had physical impairments or were emotionally upset because of a family crisis, you have no doubt experienced some of these challenges.

Cindy had such an experience on her last teaching practice, where four of the twenty-six children in her Year Two class had difficult behaviour problems. She described it this way:

> Liam and Andrew had significant learning difficulties and associated behaviour problems. They spent some time out of the classroom working individually with the learning support teacher but found it very difficult to settle when they returned and frequently disrupted the classroom activities. Although Bradley was a fluent reader and mathematically competent, he had difficulty with fine motor control, which affected his ability and interest in handwriting. During these activities he would use many disruptive behaviours to avoid the task. David had Asperger's Syndrome, which is a form of autism. He was capable of doing his work but had severe social problems which affected his willingness to concentrate, participate and interact in class. In planning the daily activities I found I had to give special consideration to strategies that would help curb or prevent possible behaviour problems for all these children.

Cindy's account showed that she developed many innovative strategies. Because she had observed that Liam and Andrew were uncertain of what to go on with when they returned to the room, she made sure that she or another child explained to them what the class activity was and had the appropriate materials ready for them. In addition to lots of encouragement and positive reinforcement, Cindy gave Bradley a generous time allowance for his handwriting, options to present oral pieces of work, and at times, arranged for all the children to work in pairs to reduce the writing load. To avoid singling David out with constant reminders about his behaviour, in the morning session, the class would decide on an appropriate rule for the day.

Within this group discussion David was pressed for suggestions to help him focus on maintaining his own behaviour. Cindy concluded her account:

> Although at times my prac experiences were flustering and frustrating, I have gained many new insights into catering for the individual needs of children. I have realized the importance and responsibility of planning, implementing and continuously evaluating the curriculum to ensure that all children's needs are being met appropriately and not just in a superficial way.

Cindy had to accept that some children in the class had difficult behaviours. She observed them closely, and tried to eliminate situations that were exacerbating the behaviour. In order to enable all children to focus on the 'what' of learning, Cindy had to focus much of her attention on 'how' issues – creating situations which would enable individual children to settle and to become more involved in their own learning. Cindy's understanding of curriculum decision making concerning the 'what' and 'how' of learning was deepened from accepting the challenge to meet a diverse range of children's needs.

Expansion of long day-care provision

The rapid expansion of long day-care provision in recent years reflects another change in society. With the increasing numbers of women with young children obtaining paid employment outside of the home, the demand for long day care has increased markedly. Although there is still some debate concerning the appropriateness of group care for very young children outside the home (Harper and Richards, 1986; Honig, 1993; Leach, 1994), there is agreement that the quality of care and education offered must be of a very high standard. This is resulting in governments, local authorities and the early childhood profession itself taking steps through regulation, accreditation or validation processes and inservice programs to establish and maintain high standards.

The provision of care and education for children over an eight- to ten-hour day, particularly for those 2 years of age and under, has raised many questions (Stonehouse, 1988). Should a distinction be made between care and education? Is it appropriate to talk about a curriculum in a long day-care setting – particularly for the birth to 2 age group? If it is acknowledged that the two questions outlined previously concerning what children need to learn and how they learn most effectively are key curriculum questions, then it would seem that curriculum is an appropriate concept for children of all ages, including babies and toddlers, whether they be in a long day-care situation or a sessional preschool programme. Agreeing on the nature of the curriculum for children in a group setting over an eight- to ten-hour day, however, is more difficult.

Rowena, who undertook her last teaching practice with the 2–3-year-old group in a day care centre found her thinking about curriculum being challenged. She said:

> In all my previous pracs I've felt it was important to have the room arranged and the activities all prepared before the children arrive. Here I've found that there are often parents and children waiting for the centre to open when I arrive with other staff for the early shift. They come in the door with us. I want to go and set the room up … but the parents have to say good-bye because they have to get to work … so it's important that I be with the children and help them feel settled. I've had to start looking at the day through the children's eyes … like … 'What's important to them?' Having the room prepared and the paints made might be important to me, but when I want to prepare … the children need a lap to cuddle into and someone who'll share a book …. From observing my supervising teacher I've discovered that I can involve them in the preparation process later. … They seem to enjoy helping make the paints as much as using them.
>
> I discovered another thing about curriculum in day care yesterday. I was working the late shift … and I was tired and the children were tired. I was getting Jock ready to go home by putting on his shoes and socks, and, to help the process I started to sing … although I didn't feel much like singing. Jock loved it … joining in and clapping his hands. He rarely joins a group for singing … and I thought then … this is more important to Jock than my planned music group time was.

Rowena was experiencing at first hand how closely intertwined care and education can be. Her previous understandings of the importance of having activities prepared and set up were being challenged as she looked at the reality of the setting through the eyes of children and responded to the needs of the children as they arose. In thinking about the 'what' of curriculum for 2–3-year-old children, Rowena was coming to understand that children are learning all the time. They are not just learning from the activities such as painting and music sessions that teachers plan for them, but from all their actions and interactions throughout the day. She realized that while teachers can influence children's learning, they certainly can't control it. She also discovered that some of the most memorable learning–teaching moments can arise spontaneously as adults respond to children's needs. Rowena was discovering yet more facets of an early childhood curriculum.

Recent developments in compulsory schooling

If you have undertaken teaching practice in a primary school you will be aware that one of the major influences impacting on early childhood curriculum for children of compulsory school age has been the trend toward a common or national curriculum. Countries like England and Wales introduced a national curriculum in 1988, while the Australian government introduced national goals for schooling in 1989 with a view to establishing a common curriculum. As a consequence, most schools work within curriculum frameworks which specify key learning areas or core and foundation subjects such as English, mathematics, science, studies of the environment and society, technology, the arts, health and physical education and languages other than English.

The introduction of a national curriculum continues to arouse much discussion and debate (Anning, 1995). Those who favour the introduction see benefits in terms of the promotion of systematic, sequential learning of distinct forms of knowledge (Aubrey, 1994). From an economic perspective, this is viewed as increasing the efficiency of teachers, with time being saved as whole-school planning meetings design programmes of study which avoid overlap of content and are in keeping with the stated goals. Others view it favourably because they see it as an attempt to ensure that a minimum level of competence in literacy and numeracy is achieved. Opponents of a common curriculum, such as Blenkin and Kelly (1988, 1994) argue, however, that there should be a developmental curriculum in order to respond to the significant differences in the ability, interests and needs of students. Other critics also maintain that the selection of particular knowledge, skills and values in a common curriculum reflects the interests of the power groups in society and that a common curriculum fails to respect the diversity of needs of students from different cultures (Crittenden, 1996). Although the debate continues, the fact is that in countries such as England and Wales legislation has been passed and early years teachers are required 'to "deliver" subject knowledge to 5–7-year-olds' (Anning, 1995: 6).

Early childhood teachers working with children of compulsory school age have had mixed reactions to these changes. Some welcome the clarity that the stated goals and objectives provide. Others, however, feel that such objectives place too much emphasis on every child's achievement of these by a certain time and fail to take into account each child's background and past experiences. Concern for subject knowledge is seen to take precedence over developmental issues. Many teachers have concerns that their approach to teaching is becoming unduly influenced by pressure to have all the children in the class achieve the stated outcomes. In other words, they feel pressured to 'teach to the test', particularly where quantifiable forms of assessment are used. As well, many feel they have been overloaded with record keeping.

Instead of emphasizing quantifiable forms of assessment some state education authorities in Australia are designing developmental continua relating to focus areas such as reading, writing and number. Use of indicators on these continua enable teachers to identify a child's phase of development. As well, they offer teachers some guidelines for helping an individual child to progress in their understanding to the next phase on the continua. In order to use the continua effectively, however, teachers have to make careful and comprehensive observations of each child and involve the children in specially designed assessment tasks. Some teachers find this form of assessment too time-consuming, while others see it as time well spent given the information it provides.

The emphasis on subject knowledge is making it more difficult for teachers to use topics or themes as a basis for their curriculum planning, although many are persisting in doing so (Cox and Sanders, 1994) because they recognize the integrated nature of young children's learning. Kym saw the benefits to be derived from integrated learning from an experience she had with a Year One class during her teaching practice. Her supervising teacher, Marta, encouraged Kym to link her curriculum content with the children's interests as much as possible. Kym wrote about her experience this way:

> My supervising teacher had prepared a unit of work based on transport. The orientating phase was completed and the children were all quite engaged in their activities and contracts. One particular day I read the children a story about a bus. It was a three-dimensional type book with movable parts. To my surprise the children became totally engrossed with this book and the song 'The Wheels on the Bus'. This interest continued for several days, with the initial direction of the unit of work changing focus. Marta suggested that we have a brainstorming session with the class so we could gauge where their interests were heading. The children said they wanted to make a bus. This idea grew, with the children deciding that they could sing the song when the bus was finished. As the class was due to present an item at the school assembly, Marta suggested they consider dramatizing the song.
>
> The children spent nearly two days making the bus, rehearsing the song and dramatizing their roles. The original work Marta had planned was disregarded – for the time being, anyway – because Marta felt it was important to follow the children's interests. All the children were involved in the construction of the bus, working on areas that interested them. I could see that they were still dealing with key areas of learning. They were using their knowledge of mathematics in measuring windows and doors and counting seats, and they had to visualize size and shape in initially designing and drawing the bus. As they worked in groups, there was much compromising and negotiating, with language being constantly used. They designed and wrote advertising posters for the sides of the bus and provided notices for the school about their assembly item. There was also much problem solving going on. Would everyone be able to hear them singing? They decided to tape themselves and play that, as well as sing with it, to increase the volume.
>
> Being a part of this experience added another dimension to my understanding of curriculum. I saw how children spontaneously integrate their learning . . . and I also saw how subjects can be integrated.

I still wonder, though, about how you know when to intervene in a child's experience to ensure that learning is occurring. With all the emphasis on learning outcomes, how can a teacher be sure children are really learning when they follow their interests like they did with the bus? I asked Marta about this. She said because she was so familiar with the curriculum content, and because she observed the children closely, she felt she was able to make reasonable judgements about the children's learning. She said that these judgements helped her to decide whether or not she needed to intervene with a particular child. I hope with more practical experience I'll become more confident in making these judgments and know when to intervene.

Kym's account of her experience with Year One children in 'integrated learning' raised some particular questions for her. Were all the children really learning? How does a teacher know if they are? Should the children's learning be focused on the key learning areas? Kym was coming to terms with yet more dimensions of the 'what' and 'how' curriculum questions as well as assessment issues. An understanding of all these dimensions is vital if you are to meet the challenges presented by a national curriculum and yet teach in a way that promotes integrated learning.

Recent developments in preschool education

What is your understanding of curriculum in preschool settings? As James's comment at the beginning of this chapter shows, many student teachers initially think of curriculum in terms of the subjects that have to be taught. In preschool settings, where children play and engage in a wide variety of activities that may not appear to be associated with subject areas, some students gain the impression, as Suzanne did, that a curriculum doesn't exist in preschool settings. Nothing could be further from the truth! Teachers of preschool-age children are vitally concerned with what young children learn and how they can learn most effectively. It would be true to say, however, that many preschool teachers talk about curriculum and go about enacting that curriculum in a very different way from many of their primary colleagues. This is because they take a developmental view of education rather than a subject-orientated view.

There are many perspectives from which you can view education. These include economic, psychological, philosophical and political perspectives. For instance, given the considerable funding required by education, including services for children under school age, an economic argument can be put that a common curriculum which specifies outcomes is likely to be the most cost efficient. The introduction of preschool curriculum guidelines in some countries in recent years, together with demands for teachers to be more accountable, is seen to stem from such an economic perspective. Some preschool teachers are concerned that their developmental approach to curriculum may be threatened if these guidelines place emphasis on the achievement of identified learning outcomes which are more subject-orientated than developmentally based. Before you can assess whether there are grounds for these concerns you need to understand what a developmental view of education is.

A developmental perspective places the focus on the child as the learner and the constructor of knowledge. It is derived from developmental theorists such as Piaget, Freud, Erikson, Vygotsky, Bruner and Kohlberg (see Sebastian–Nickell and Milne, 1992, for a summary of their theories). These developmental theorists believe that a child has an innate capacity to learn. Recent brain research (Caine and Caine, 1990) has confirmed this innate search for meaning and the brain's natural capacity to integrate information by constantly perceiving meanings and generating conceptual patterns. The child is seen as continually developing and changing, moving from one stage to the next more complex stage. This developmental view requires a teacher to match learning experiences with the level of a child's emerging abilities. For example, instruction about telling the time, the calendar, and calculating arithmetically before a child is able to understand these concepts, can result in children losing confidence in their own abilities to think. On the other hand, a teacher must also be able to gauge a child's abilities in order to challenge and extend learning (De Vries and Kohlberg, 1990).

The learning process is seen to be a creative activity, with the learning content being stamped with the child's own unique view of the world. Given this constructive view of learning, it makes no sense to talk of learning as being separate from content (Elkind, 1989). For instance, with young children there is little point in talking about teaching thinking or problem-solving skills as separate areas of learning. These skills are learned as children engage in real situations where real problems arise and have to be solved. A child's conception of content will always be influenced by the child's own way of making sense of the world. For instance, a 4-year-old who, after intently watching an aeroplane take off, asks if the people inside will get bigger again when the aeroplane lands is seeing the world very differently from his 8-year-old brother.

From a developmental perspective, the aim of education is to produce 'creative, inventive discoverers ... to form minds which can be critical, can verify, and not accept everything that is offered' (Piaget, 1964, cited in Elkind, 1989: 115). Developmentalists argue that the way to do this is to create learning environments that are developmentally appropriate. By this stage you may be wondering what developmentally appropriate environments are and how you create them.

The position paper on Developmentally Appropriate Practice (Bredekamp, 1987), known as DAP in its abbreviated form, outlines how these environments are created. Produced by the National Association for the Education of Young Children in the United States in response to concerns regarding the trend towards more formal and academic teaching of very young children, the position paper seeks to highlight practices drawn from developmental theory that are appropriate to the age of the child as well as being responsive to a child's individual and cultural needs (Bredekamp and Rosegrant, 1992).

Although the statement on DAP has been generally accepted by early childhood teachers, who have used it to justify many aspects of their curriculum, it has also fuelled much debate amongst academic writers and has been criticized for its over-reliance on developmental theory, its reliance on Western cultural attitudes, and its failure to recognize the interconnectedness between the child, the family and society (Cross, 1995). Another major criticism stemming from DAP's reliance on child development theory is that, although it can tell us *how* to teach, it cannot be used to tell us *what should be taught* to young children (Spodek, 1991, 1993). While in one sense this is true, in that knowledge of development cannot tell us what knowledge society deems to be of value, Elkind (1989) and Katz (1996) maintain that, in another sense, knowledge of development does assist teachers in deciding on content because it indicates what is appropriate for a child's particular stage of development.

The introduction of preschool curriculum guidelines has refuelled the debate concerning the 'what' of preschool curriculum, and raised questions concerning how decisions are made when selecting the 'what' of curriculum. It is interesting to note that the 'areas of learning' or 'learning outcomes' identified in recent preschool curriculum guidelines in England and Wales and several Australian states focus on areas relating to personal and social development, language and literacy, mathematics and technology, knowledge and understanding of the world, health and physical development, creative development and thinking skills. Apart from the particular emphasis on personal and social development, most of these learning areas seem similar to the learning areas designated for higher levels of schooling. Indeed, the document on nursery education, *Desirable Outcomes for Children's Learning*, by the School Curriculum and Assessment Authority in England, shows how the outcomes specified link with Levels 1 and 2 of the National Curriculum. It would seem, then, that decisions concerning the 'what' of preschool curriculum content and the consequent desired outcomes are being influenced by decisions concerning curriculum content at higher levels of education. While this has been described negatively as the downward escalation of curriculum (Shepard and Smith, 1986), it can also be viewed more positively in terms of promoting continuity, provided that children are enabled to make the transition gradually by building on what they know as they become acquainted with the more formalized subject areas.

In the light of these considerations, do you think preschool teachers have grounds for concern regarding their developmental approach to teaching? While there is some evidence (Hatch, 1988) to suggest that pressures to achieve particular outcomes can influence early childhood teachers to use more direct instructional methods, another study (Fisher, 1993) has indicated that where a teacher's beliefs in a developmental approach to learning and teaching are sufficiently strong, principles of developmental practice can be implemented while meeting the requirements of the national curriculum. Suzanne's account of her teaching practice experiences reflect these latter findings.

Both teaching practice settings experienced by Suzanne were in the public education system, where curriculum content was prescribed in terms of key learning areas. The teachers' actions and the children's experiences in each classroom were, however, very different. In the first setting the teacher focused solely on content or subject matter without considering the children and the way they learn. As a consequence the children experienced whole-class teaching, and learning was 'isolated' and lacked personal meaning. In contrast, in the second situation, the teacher took a developmental approach, seeing the children as active learners. The content was incorporated into the children's activity, linked to previous knowledge and had personal meaning for the children.

It is interesting to wonder why these two teachers were so different in their teaching approaches. What factors were influencing their decision making? Was it that they held different beliefs about learning and teaching, or was it that the teacher in the first setting was so influenced by the demands of the system in terms of content and outcomes that it dominated her teaching approach? It could be suggested that the second teacher, while teaching the prescribed *content*, was using *processes* that were consistent with her own knowledge and beliefs about developmental learning and her knowledge of individual children, and matching her *intentions* with those of the children. She not only knew *what* to teach, but also *why* the content should be taught in a certain way. De Vries and Kohlberg (1990: 380) maintain that teachers who hold convictions about teaching based on a theoretical rationale have autonomy – 'They think about whether they agree with what is suggested. They take responsibility for the education they are offering children.'

These reflections suggest, then, that early childhood teachers who want to take a developmental approach to curriculum – who believe that it is important to take principles from child development into account when making decisions about children, content and teaching strategies – will still be able to do so while working towards the goals and outcomes specified in curriculum guidelines. It must be recognized, however, that there are many factors influencing curriculum decisions, and that teachers may feel pressured not only from within their education system, but also by parents, the school and the wider community to focus more on the specific content in order to meet 'set' requirements. If, however, you decide that you want to take a developmental approach while at the same time meeting the demands of the education system and society, you will need to clarify your own views about learning and teaching and fully understand their practical implications.

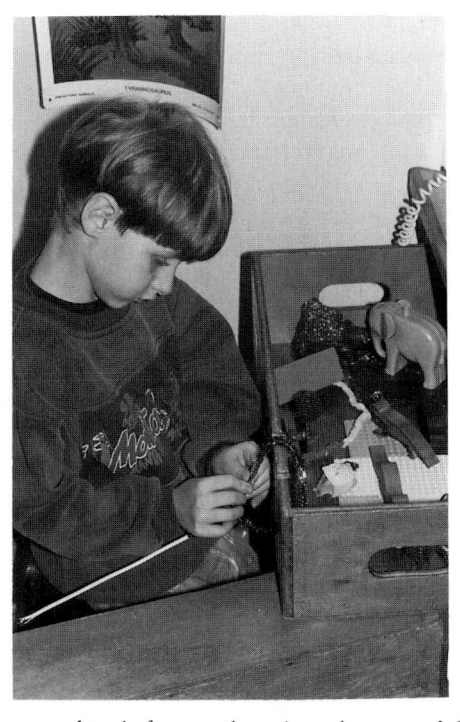

Plate 3.2 Is setting up an electric fence to keep intruders out of the wild-life park he
has created a legitimate aspect of this child's curriculum?
(Photo courtesy of Northgate State Preschool.)

DEVELOPING BELIEFS ABOUT CHILDREN, LEARNING AND TEACHING

When you become a teacher, regardless of the age of the children with whom
you work, you will be faced with making curriculum decisions about what
children learn and how they can be helped to learn most effectively. Whether
you are expected to work within curriculum frameworks or not, your own
experiences, your knowledge derived from your readings and personal beliefs
about children, about learning and about teaching will be a part of your
decision making (Spodek, 1988). It is therefore vital that you begin to clarify
what you know and believe and to develop your own philosophy – your own
ideas – of teaching.

You may be interested to read Kay's statement of her philosophy. She
wrote this at the end of her course as she was preparing her job applications:

Introductory statement: From birth, children are establishing themselves as social beings, firstly as members of their families and then as
members of a larger community. They use the language they acquire

and draw upon their experiences to practise and consolidate communicative and problem-solving skills. The children's existing interests and abilities are extended and refined as they form concepts of themselves as social beings, communicators, creators and problem solvers. These concepts will determine their views of their own abilities and worth, and, in the longer term, influence their attitudes towards learning, towards themselves and towards others. For these reasons,

I believe that, as an early childhood teacher, I have a very special responsibility to the young children and their families with whom I work.

I see my role as an early childhood teacher being influenced by my beliefs about children and learning.

I believe that:

- Children are unique individuals, with their own timing of social, emotional, cognitive and physical growth and development.
- Children not only have individual personalities and learning styles, but also unique experiences stemming from their family and cultural backgrounds which are to be valued equally.
- Children learn through an interactive process between their thoughts and experiences with materials, ideas, adults and other children and by using all their senses.
- Children's play has an important role in facilitating their social, emotional, cognitive and physical development.
- Children learn when they have positive self-esteem and are in an environment where there is mutual respect and cooperation.

I believe that children's learning and development is promoted when:

- an integrated, individualized curriculum provides for children's interests and a range of development, supports curiosity and the exploration of ideas;
- activities are child centred, match children's abilities, and foster a variety of individual and group experiences;
- materials and resources provided are meaningful, developmentally appropriate and contain no bias towards a specific gender, race or religion;
- parents, families and carers are encouraged to participate in their children's learning and when strong home–school links are established and maintained;
- children feel comfortable and secure and have a sense of ownership in their learning environment;
- there is rhythm and routine to the day, with flexibility to cater for unexpected episodes;
- all children have opportunities to experience language, problem solving and creativity.

If you were writing a personal statement of your philosophy would you outline similar beliefs to Kay's, or would they be different? Do you think it's important to take into account the views of the families and the community in which you will be working? Would you want to add more on the 'what' of learning to your statement? If the task of developing your own statement of beliefs seems too difficult for you at this stage, delve into some of the many early childhood textbooks that focus on developmental curriculum (for instance, Hendrick, 1990; Kostelnik *et al.*, 1993; Moyles, 1992; Wortham, 1994), as these could help you clarify your ideas. It is vital that, as you seek to clarify your ideas about curriculum and educational philosophies, you do your own thinking and consider what you are reading in the light of your own experiences and values. If you fail to do this you will end up with a statement of other people's beliefs which will be of little use to you! You need to develop your own vision of what you want the curriculum to be for the children in your class.

TRANSFORMING CURRICULUM VISIONS INTO ACTIONS THAT REALIZE THE VISIONS

After reading the heading to this section you are probably saying, 'Get real!' I admit that transforming visions into reality does seem an almost impossible task, but, in fact, when you are dealing with what might seem very basic and down-to-earth questions regarding your practice teaching you are clarifying your visions so that you can develop actions in order to realize them. Some students were asking such questions in a tutorial leading up to their period of teaching practice recently.

For instance, Jo indicated her concerns about planning for the toddler group. She said: 'I'm doing my next prac in a day-care centre. I know how to plan for older preschoolers but how do I plan for the toddler group?'

Melanie was concerned about the requirement that she plan for children in her second week. She commented: 'I have to plan for the children in the preschool group in my second week of prac. Getting to know them takes time . . . so how do I plan while I'm getting to know them?'

Penny was worried about her first teaching practice in a primary school. With some hesitation she said: 'I know this sounds a silly question but what do you actually teach in a Year One class? Do I have to focus on the content prescribed in the curriculum documents, or can I follow the children's interests like I did on my preschool prac?'

As we went about finding some answers to these questions it was apparent that each student had a 'picture' of what and how they wanted children to learn. They were not sure, however, how to bring that picture alive – how to turn their ideal into reality. This led to a discussion of the role of planning and how translating some ideals or aims into achievable objectives can assist.

Planning for the under 3s

In discussing how to plan for toddlers the students first shared their vision of curriculum for this age group. This suggested toddlers being responded to with warmth and hugs – being surrounded with a sense of security, yet being encouraged to explore and to touch – playing alongside others – participating in interesting sensory experiences – their physical needs being met – their parents' views taken into account. Fiona, who had undertaken a practicum in a toddler group, shared her thoughts about her planning experiences. She said:

> Well ... it isn't like the planning you do for preschool children. I feel like you've got to seize the moment and go with what's happening. At my preschool prac I could write a plan for the day and generally I was able to carry it through ... but with toddlers you can only have a broad plan. And I think you've really got to get to know the children ... and then when those moments arise you know how to respond ... you know the ones you can encourage to be more independent ... and the ones with the short attention spans. You think, 'Get in there, now, while they're doing something.' Like one day when we were playing with the 'put together blocks' ... the children can just put them together ... or you can start to talk about the pictures on the blocks with them .... Andrew just didn't seem to want to play with anything ... he just watched. All the other kids were standing around the blocks ... and Andrew started to reach out for them ... just pointing ... so I gave him a block ... and then he began to pick them up and give them to me. So I think its things like that you've got to think of in planning for this age group.
>
> I guess I had aims for Andrew ... to start to play with some toys ... and to play alongside other children, but I couldn't plan a set activity because Andrew wouldn't have been interested. I just had to respond when Andrew indicated he was interested in the blocks. I guess you have to have the right environment for that to happen ... and you have to plan that environment too.

Getting to know the children through observing them closely and interacting with them helped Fiona develop some broad aims for each child. In order to achieve them, however, she had to 'seize the moment'. This meant having a close relationship with the children so she would be sensitive to that moment and their responses. The moment was also made possible by the provision of an interesting yet relaxed environment. Planning how you will organize and present the environment is therefore also vital if your curriculum visions are to be realized.

Planning for 3–5-year-olds

All students in the tutorial agreed with Melanie that it was difficult to plan effectively for preschool children before knowing them well. I shared with them how Tania had attempted to overcome this difficulty in her teaching practice with a group of 4–5-year-olds. In her first week at the centre Tania had observed that five of the children had a very strong friendship group and spent most of their time outdoors together. They did not welcome other children into their games and, when approached, 'ganged up' to exclude them. The 'excluded' children came up to Tania and the supervising teacher on several occasions complaining that no one would play with them. Although the other 'excluded' children were not unduly upset by this, Nicole persisted in wanting to join the group and became increasingly upset about her exclusion.

In thinking about the situation Tania used her knowledge of child development. She had observed that Nicole's feeling of being rejected was beginning to affect her view of herself adversely. Although she did not know the history of 'the gang', she recognized that something needed to be done to rectify the situation. In keeping with her own vision of a preschool curriculum she also wanted the children to show more concern for one another and to be aware of how their actions could affect others. In the light of these considerations Tania made plans, enacted them and then made her evaluation (see Table 3.1).

Although Tania did not know each child particularly well after only one week, in making decisions about how to handle the situation she was influenced by her general views of the children as learners. Her objectives, for example, suggest that she saw them as problem solvers, capable of expressing their thoughts and ideas at their level of understanding. She also saw thinking and content as being closely related, with the development of problem-solving skills being fostered as the children dealt with a 'real' problem.

'But', the students in the tutorial asked, 'how did Tania get the idea to introduce the discussion with a letter?' I had wondered that, too, and when I asked her she said she had seen a video where a teacher had used a similar technique to start a discussion. She had been fascinated by the way the children had responded by expressing so many ideas, and had jotted down the technique so she could try it for herself. When she was thinking about how she could discuss the problem without making Nicole feel worse, she had remembered this technique and thought it seemed a useful way of approaching the problem indirectly.

Tania's evaluations of the children's responses suggest that the letter was a useful stimulus for promoting the objectives she had set and that the open-ended nature of the activity had enabled the children to respond at their level of ability. In writing down some examples of what the children said or

Table 3.1 Extract from Tania's planning book

Objectives	Teaching strategies	Evaluation
To encourage children to show concern for others To encourage children to express their ideas and thoughts To pose a real problem for the children to solve To help children develop problem solving techniques in an indirect manner	Introduce discussion by showing and reading children a 'letter' I received from a girl I had taught at another preschool. Dear Miss Willcox I have a problem and I was wondering if you could help me. My problem is that I have no one to play with. Sometimes when I do start playing with other children they tell me to go away. I am very sad. What do your preschoolers think I should do? Can you please write back and tell me? Love Melissa Encourage children to share ideas about what Melissa could do.	The letter aroused much interest. The children were genuinely concerned about Melissa and her problem, and suggested that Melissa should come to our preschool. Seth said she could go and tell the teacher. Other comments were: – she could tell the children that's not a very nice way to talk, and they should let her play – she could just play by herself – she could tell the children that she doesn't want to play with them if they are going to be mean – she could do the same back to them. We discussed each of these solutions to see which ones were useful to Melissa. We decided that we should write to Melissa and say that she should tell the children she would like to play with them, and if they say 'No' then she should say, 'That's not a very nice thing to say,' or 'I don't like it when you talk to me like that,' or 'We should all be friends and play together'. Nicole just sat and listened to the whole discussion. I feel the children did really think about how to solve the problem using solutions that many of them tend to use. It will be interesting to observe whether this discussion has any effect.

suggested in her evaluation Tania was able to reflect more deeply on the nature of their thinking. In considering Tania's example, the students in the tutorial agreed that by drawing on her existing knowledge about children as well as her ideals, Tania had shown that effective planning and action can be undertaken as you are getting know individual children.

Planning for 5–8-year-olds

From the discussions earlier in this chapter, you know that thinking about planning in a Year One classroom involves dealing with how to focus on prescribed content while at the same time taking into account the needs of individual learners and building on their prior knowledge. Because we ran out of time in the tutorial we agreed to discuss Penny's question the following week. A number of students who had previously undertaken teaching practice in primary settings agreed to share their planning experiences. Melinda was the first volunteer, and she described how she had linked prescribed content with children's interests through what is variously described as a topic, unit or thematic approach (Bredekamp, 1991; Kostelnik *et al.*, 1993).

Melinda said that her supervising teacher suggested that she be totally responsible for planning in the third week of her teaching practice. Melinda decided to build the learning activities for the week around the topic 'When the circus comes to town'. This was because the children had been discussing animals, and some children had mentioned that the circus was their favourite place, so she felt it linked with their current interests. She discussed the curriculum web she had developed, which showed how related concepts could be incorporated into all the key learning areas.

In order to recall her feelings and experiences accurately, Melinda shared some of her journal entries with the tutorial group. She had written:

Table 3.2 Melinda's curriculum web, 'When the circus comes to town'

Science	*English*	*Maths*
Investigate circus animals: • what animals? • why these animals? • what do they eat?	Write a letter to a friend about the circus Poem – 'Circus circus' Talk about the jobs of circus people Think of words to do	How many people are coming to the circus? Money: entry price for each child's family? Marching band: how many
Art Design a poster Draw favourite animal Make clown faces Create ringmaster's hat Make money	with 'circus' beginning with 'b' and 'p' Research circuses Read other stories about the circus Write a circus program	pairs of boots needed? Patterns for clown outfits Calculating/predicting food
Music Band instruments: drums cymbals, recorder, triangle Sing circus songs	*Social studies* Think about life in circus (people/animals) Relationships between people and animals Responsibilities to animals Ringmaster's role (can be a girl)	*Drama* Marching band: how to march Movement: putting up tent Pretend you're an animal Have a performance

I feel like a real teacher planning an entire week's work. I think the curriculum web is OK, but my daily plans might be a bit ambitious. I do want to incorporate the children's ideas as well. I think I might have to tone down the related activities a little. Mrs D has approved my plans which is really exciting. I am getting such a BUZZ!

In her daily programme Melinda had planned how to involve the children in sharing and developing their knowledge of circuses as well as integrating the topic with the key learning areas.

Daily plan, Tuesday, 7 May

9.00–9.30	Assembly
9.30–10.00	Library
10.00	

1 Read 'When the circus comes to town' by Brenda Parkes.
2 Discuss circuses . . . encourage children's input . . . think about the people and the animals who could be in the circus. Could we create a circus?
3 Children to write about who they would like to be in the circus (ringmaster, acrobat, lion tamer, clowns, ticket seller, animals . . .) and draw picture.
4 Reflection as a group (Who did each decide to be? why? who were the same?)

11.30

5 Group the children according to the roles they had decided upon.
('Discover' roles for children who may not have decided.)
6 Tally how many in each group.
7 Sequencing . . . discuss what needs to be done in setting up a circus
first – decide who is in it
second – decide on name
third – decide how much it will cost to see the circus. Different prices adults/children?
fourth – decide on the acts
fifth – advertise.
8 Make money.

12.30

9 Read story about one of the animals in the circus.

2.00

10 Group children. Get them to discuss costumes . . . something they could make for their costume.

In discussing her experiences with the tutorial group Melinda again referred to her journal entries:

May 7

I introduced my plan today. It worked! The children were very enthusiastic, adding lots of their ideas. They were even chatting about the circus in the playground at lunch time. The children have made most of the choices so far. Tomorrow we are deciding on a name for the circus. (They are thinking about it overnight.) We have an acrobatic troupe, some clowns, some animals and even a juggler.

May 8

I mentioned that my circus ideas might be a little ambitious – seems so! The 'practice' session got out of hand today. Although the practice session went well yesterday it wasn't the same today. Three children were hurt (not badly) in the space of a few minutes. I dealt with this by stopping the practice session and discussing the problem with the children. We decided to make a list of rules for the circus so that everyone's safety was assured. I should have done this in the first place. Tomorrow the practice session will be held in the activity centre to avoid the problem of lack of space.

The children thought very hard about names for the circus. We ended up with 'The Scary Acrobat Circus'. It felt good knowing that I was incorporating maths into the process of naming the circus. We voted and represented votes with tally marks using the tally symbol for five. Madeline did well during maths. I asked about admission prices to the circus. I said, 'If someone paid Stuart (our money taker) $9, how many people would be going in to the circus? Madeline answered correctly that it would be one adult and two children (prices = $5 adults, $2 children). Mrs D gave me some constructive criticism about my strategies today which I will take on board tomorrow.

May 9

The children worked on their circus posters this morning. Most children had their own ideas, so the posters are all different with some interesting border patterns. I felt each child used the space com-petently. They also enjoyed themselves. They told me they did! This is probably the most important aspect of all to achieve.

May 10

The circus became a production today with a real audience – parents. The children arrived with costumes and we spent time preparing the classroom and the performers! The circus itself was more a concert with circus acts. On reflection, it would have been useful for the children to have watched a circus performance on video. Although they could talk about aspects of the circus, not many of the children had concepts of the processes involved as few had actually been to a real circus. Unfortunately, this realization came too late. Still they enjoyed themselves, and learned a lot. I have learned many things too... that I can implement a week's planning using my ideas and the children's ideas; that I can succeed in challenging children; and that I can tap into and use their interests to benefit their learning. I have also learned more about children: what they like; their humour; and how they learn.

Melinda's approach to planning offered her a way of focusing on the prescribed content in all the key learning areas in a context that was of interest to the children and which enabled them to explore and develop new concepts. The processes of learning -expressing thoughts and ideas, making choices, negotiating, reaching decisions, making rules – were an integral part of the content, yet matched with Melinda's beliefs that children should be actively involved and enjoying their own learning.

A FRAMEWORK FOR DECISION MAKING

From the examples of these three students' experiences in planning it is evident that, regardless of the age group they were working with, their curriculum work involved them in making decisions. They each had to:

- *decide to act* (e.g., Fiona – to engage the toddler Andrew with materials; Tania – to try to overcome the adverse effects 'the gang' was having on Nicole's self-esteem; Melinda – to design a curriculum topic for Year One children);
- *decide how to act* (e.g., Fiona – to give a toddler security, but encourage playfulness; Tania – to provide relevant experiences which matched the learners' needs and her objectives for the group and Nicole; Melinda – to guide classroom behaviour while teaching prescribed content in ways that encouraged active participation and choice);
- *decide whether or not actions were effective* (e.g., in all the examples students observed, noted and reflected on the children's responses in order to understand their thinking and behaviour better, as well as considering the children's responses in relation to their objectives).

This is a simple framework for curriculum decision making which you may like to use. In making these decisions you will find yourself drawing on your beliefs about children and the way they learn, and on your 'picture' of the kind of experiences you want children to have. As you reflect on whether or not your decisions and actions were effective in achieving your objectives, you will also begin to clarify some of the many things a teacher does in enacting an early childhood curriculum. It has been suggested (Katz, 1987) that the role of the teacher in an early childhood curriculum is:

- to engage children in active rather than passive activities;
- to help children understand their social and physical worlds;
- to assist children in respecting their own rights and feelings as well as those of others;
- to intervene in order to establish more desirable behaviour patterns;
- to create trusting environments where children share their ideas and thoughts;
- to create contexts where learning has a purpose and real problems are solved;
- to make decisions that take into account both the immediate and long-term benefits of experiences;
- to be flexible and use a variety of teaching strategies.

If you think about the decisions and actions taken by Fiona, Tania and Melinda, you will see that they were doing many of these things. They were dealing with content, processes and intentions in turning their ideals into reality.

SUMMARY

Throughout this chapter curriculum has been presented as a concept which is dynamic in nature, has many facets, and means different things to different people. Although curriculum is often thought of in terms of the content to be taught, it is vital that you also think of curriculum in terms of the processes that relate to learning and teaching, the intentions that both you and the learner hold, as well as the realities that arise from classroom interactions and situations. You need to consider these facets along with the content when planning and enacting the curriculum because they all affect children's learning.

As you undertake teaching practice in different settings across the early years you will become aware that changes in society are being reflected in these settings. For instance, with an increasingly diverse population a growing number of children with a wide range of needs must be catered for by teachers. Similarly, the introduction of national curriculum frameworks for compulsory schooling, curriculum guidelines for preschools and accreditation processes in day-care centres are placing greater demands on teachers in terms of accountability and the attainment of prescribed outcomes. Being aware of these trends and the debates they have raised concerning the 'what' and 'how' of curriculum, as well as the nature of appropriate assessment for young children, is important, because, as a teacher, you will have to decide how you are going to meet your professional responsibilities. Even though the content or outcomes may be prescribed by an external source, the ways in which these 'requirements' are met depend on 'how' the teacher plans and organizes the environment for learning. Your beliefs about children, learning and teaching then become very important because they influence the nature of your planning, decision making and actions.

SUGGESTED ACTIVITIES

- Think of two or three memorable experiences or conversations you have had with young children. Describe them to a friend and together discuss what they suggest or indicate about the ways in which young children learn or think. Consider your role in the situation. Did your contribution assist the learning process? How?

- Before you undertake teaching practice, write a brief statement of your beliefs about how young children learn and what you see the role of the teacher to be. After teaching practice, review your statement. Make changes if your views have changed or note if your views have been strengthened by your experiences. This is an interesting exercise to undertake at different times during your pre-service education as it documents how your understandings are clarified and extended. (Thinking of a metaphor or drawing a picture of your current understanding of an early childhood curriculum – the teacher's role – or the nature of children's learning, can also be a valuable exercise.)

- After teaching practice, share with a friend two examples of successful learning experiences to which you contributed. Using the decision-making framework suggested in this chapter, discuss why you decided to act, how you planned and acted on those plans, and why you decided that your actions were effective. Suggest ways you could have made the experience even more succesful.

- You are preparing for a job interview. There are parents from the centre or school on the panel, and you anticipate that they will ask you about your philosophy of early childhood education. Prepare your reply in a written form and then role play the interview situation. Respond verbally to such questions as:

  'What do you think our children will gain from attending your preschool class?'
  'I want to be sure my Sarah will learn to read and write and be able to do maths. How will you go about teaching her to do that in Year One?'
  'I'm not sure our 2-year-old, Tom, will cope with being with other children. Do you expect them to socialize?'

- You have been appointed to teach a class of 5–6-year-olds from the beginning of the school year and you have been told that there are several children from culturally diverse backgrounds in the group. From your readings and discussions with other students and teachers describe a number of strategies that you would use to help these children feel welcome, valued and included, and outline why you chose these strategies.

- Debate the statement, 'In a "good" early childhood curriculum it is more important that young children be curious and active in their own learning than to be given specific information and facts.'

4

CREATING
ENVIRONMENTS FOR
LEARNING AND TEACHING

In this chapter ways of developing effective environments for learning and teaching will be considered by:

- thinking about the organization of the physical aspects of the setting;
- becoming aware of the 'messages' and effects of different forms of organization;
- recognizing the links between beliefs about learning and teaching and organizational decisions;
- reflecting on the importance of preparation;
- considering factors that promote a supportive social climate.

ORGANIZING THE PHYSICAL ENVIRONMENT: WHAT'S INVOLVED?

A few months after the start of the school year I was chatting with Joy, a teacher who had only recently graduated and taken up a position teaching 4–5-year-olds. She was keen to share her experiences of the first few weeks. She said:

> When I saw that bare empty preschool room with all the furniture stacked on one side . . . I freaked out. My mind went a complete blank and I thought, 'I'll never organize this.' On my previous pracs the rooms were all set up and organized and I hadn't given much thought as to how or why they functioned so smoothly. When I stopped being in such a panic I thought back to my last prac and how Mrs J arranged her room . . . and I realized that, with a few variations to take account of the doors and fixed cupboards, I could arrange my room in much the same way.

Joy's experience is an important reminder of the need to think about the factors that contribute to the effective functioning of an early childhood setting. Because you generally undertake teaching practice at a time when your supervising teacher has arranged the physical environment and settled the children into the routines, it is possible to remain unaware, as Joy did, of the many factors that need to be considered in order to create a smooth-functioning learning environment. There are a number of steps you can take during each teaching practice to help you be better prepared to organize your classroom when you obtain a teaching position. These steps include:

- becoming aware of the different ways in which key aspects of the physical environment can be organized;
- considering how different arrangements and provisions affect the children's responses and behaviours;
- examining the possible reasons for particular organizational decisions;
- proposing alternative arrangements for particular situations;
- thinking about the messages that result from organizational decisions.

Key aspects of the physical environment

During teaching practice, you are usually so busy observing and interacting with children that you have little time to consider the physical features of the room or playground. It is important that you make time to consider these physical factors, however, because a number of studies (Phyfe-Perkins, 1980; Phyfe-Perkins and Shoemaker, 1986; Smith and Connolly, 1980) have shown that the way in which the environment is arranged and organized does affect the behaviour of the children and adults within it.

There are a number of ways you can build your awareness of important physical aspects. You can become familiar with the design features, aesthetic aspects, and forms of organization including time schedules, which textbooks (for example, Bronson, 1995; Greenman, 1988; Hendrick, 1990; Moyles, 1992; Walsh, 1988) suggest contribute to effective learning environments. You can also note the environmental features of your teaching practice settings by making sketches, or, with your supervising teacher's permission, taking photographs of the room plans, furniture arrangements, playground designs, storage provision and aesthetic features. As well, writing down the schedule of the day and noting how this relates to the particular circumstances of the setting can provide you with a valuable base for the development of your own ideas. You may find it interesting to compare the physical features and form of organization you have noted with the information and recommended forms of organization suggested in textbooks. Some key aspects of the physical environment are:

- the arrangement and use of space and equipment;
- the selection and storage of materials;
- the schedule of the day.

For a recent tutorial I asked some final year students to bring a sample of the records and photographs that they had collected from their various practice teaching experiences so that we could share and discuss their observations and impressions. Reading their observations and comments may help you be more alert to some of the physical factors that may be influencing the children, and you, in your teaching practice setting.

The arrangement and use of space and equipment

After looking at the sketches and photographs and listening to one another's comments, the students realized that there was wide variation in the use of space and the arrangement of equipment in early childhood settings. For instance, some lower primary classrooms had desks grouped into fours, a carpeted space for group discussion as well as other inviting activity, or interest areas containing computers, collage and art materials, blocks and manipulative materials, maths games and books. Other classrooms appeared far more austere with all desks facing the chalk board, books and number games placed on shelves but not displayed, and children's work folders for different subjects prominently stored. In some schools there were separate adventure playgrounds for the younger children, while other schools had no such provision.

Similarly, preschool settings varied in appearance. In some, activities provided by the teacher were set out on tables, with areas for home play, painting, blocks, puzzles and manipulative equipment being clearly defined. In other preschools there were large open spaces in which children con-structed buildings such as 'houses', 'boats', or 'hospitals for sick animals' before playing in them. In some preschools, blocks were stored on fixed shelves and could only be played with on the carpet, while in others, blocks were stored on non-tippable, mobile trolleys and placed around the room near to the 'building sites'. Some preschool teachers required that all equipment be packed away at the end of the session, while others arranged for buildings and games to be left up so that play could be continued and further developed in the next session.

The selection and storage of materials

After sharing their information concerning materials and equipment the students also agreed that settings differed markedly in terms of the quality and quantity of materials available, as well as in the ways in which the materials were provided and stored. Sylvia, for instance, said that in her day-care centre there was a good supply of equipment for the under 3s which she felt catered for all areas of their development. For children's social and pretend play there were dress-up clothes, as well as dolls with simple clothes for dressing, and a variety of animal and people figures and transport vehicles to use with blocks or sand. There were materials such as fit-in puzzles and simple matching and sorting games which encouraged exploration and problem solving and a large collection of sturdy books. Other materials such as simple instruments, scarves and dancing accessories promoted music and movement, while a supply of art materials encouraged visual expression. An adjustable, low climbing structure, ride-on and wheeled toys, balls and materials for sand and water play were available for fine and gross motor activity. Other centres for the under 3s, however, had minimal equipment available, and students commented that this often resulted in friction because children of this age group were not able to cope easily with sharing and turn taking.

Students were surprised at the different ways in which materials were made available to children, particularly for the 4–8-year-olds. For instance, in some settings children had access to a wide range of materials which were stored in open shelving units around the room or in an open storeroom adjoining the main activity area. Photographs of these storerooms showed that re-cyclable materials such as small plastic coils and spools, pieces of leather and cardboard, boxes, artificial flowers, furniture factory off-cuts and the like were stored in clearly labelled and colour-coded boxes. The colour coding enabled children to return the red box to its rightful place on the bottom shelf where all the other red boxes were stored. Materials that teachers did not want children to access daily were kept on high shelves out of the children's reach.

Several students had noted that teachers varied in their expectations concerning the children's use of equipment. Although James had worked with several teachers who required children to read the books in the book area, and to use the scissors and masking tape at the making table, his last teaching practice had been with a teacher who let the children use the equipment or materials where they were needed. Provided the children treated the materials with respect and had a reason for wanting them, they could be taken anywhere in the room. James told of how a child was able to take some puzzles into his hospital so that the sick children would have something to do.

The schedule of the day

In sharing their examples of daily schedules a number of students indicated that they had discovered that developing a schedule was more than just filling in time slots. Various factors had to be taken into consideration depending on the setting and age groups of the children concerned. For instance, teachers in primary classes had to consider the schedule of other specialist teachers and work around times for visits to the library and classes with the music and physical education teachers as well as school assemblies. Having specific times for morning tea and lunch breaks also meant that lessons and activities tended to end abruptly rather than flow on if the children were actively engaged. Gaynor had realized the importance of planning around these times after experiencing the frustration of having the lunch bell go just as the children were totally absorbed in discussing the jobs that would need to be done on 'the farm' that the class was creating.

Three students who had undertaken teaching practice in long day-care settings highlighted some of the complexities they had discovered were associated with developing a daily schedule for the under 3s. In sharing their experiences they compiled a list of factors which they felt had to be taken into account in developing a flexible yet predictable daily schedule. These factors included:

- being able to respond immediately to toddlers' needs;
- avoiding waiting times;
- adapting the length of activities to individual children's attention spans;
- providing some regular routines and rituals relating to meals and rest;
- allowing for unhurried one-to-one interactions between children and staff to foster language and the building of relationships;
- the varying staff–child ratios at particular times of the day;
- timing the use of the playground if it is shared with older children;
- allowing time to talk with the children's parents at arrival and departure times.

Some students raised the question of how to provide for a balance of activity in terms of time. For instance, in preschool settings should the same amount of time be spent indoors as outdoors? What amount of time should be spent in whole-group situations compared with the time spent in individual or small-group activity? Sarah told of her experience with a preschool group who spent more time indoors on some days but then balanced this by having a longer period outdoors on other days. She indicated that the children were often involved in the decisions with their teacher about where they would play and what time they would spend there.

These observations and comments indicate that there are many factors that can separately, and in combination, influence children's experiences in early childhood settings. You will no doubt discover many more factors once you start to look at the way your teaching practice setting operates and is organized. It is not enough to just note these factors, however. You also have to consider the ways in which they influence the experiences children have.

CONSIDERING THE MESSAGES AND EFFECTS OF THE PHYSICAL ORGANIZATION

Towards the end of the tutorial we began to talk about *how* children could be affected by the physical organization of the setting. As the students thought about this question, Jane recalled that her supervising teacher had said that she thought of arranging her room in terms of the messages she wanted to send to children. If you view organization in this way then the physical arrangement of the setting becomes a matter of great importance, because:

- it sends messages to children about what they are expected to do;
- it has consequences for children in terms of what they can do.

Do you think that the way in which a room is arranged sends messages to children? In a room where puzzles, threading, potato prints and lacing boards are set out on tables it seems likely that children will get the message, 'There are certain tasks you are expected to undertake here.' In a room where there are cardboard boxes and blocks, dress-up clothes, space for building and a storeroom which children are able to access, however, it seems more likely that children will get the message, 'Here is a place where you can play and act on your own ideas.' I told the students about a visit I had made to a preschool in the first week of the school year. Just inside the door the teacher had placed a small table and chairs. A bright cloth covered the table and it was set with plastic plates, cups and saucers, spoons and a teapot. A teddybear and a doll sat on two of the chairs. A child only had to take a step into this room to get the message that here was a place to play. This teacher strongly believed that the room arrangement signalled a message.

The type of materials available and the ways they are presented also send messages to children and have consequences in terms of what children can do. If children can only use the coloured pieces of paper set out on the table to decorate their boxes, then they don't have to make too many choices or

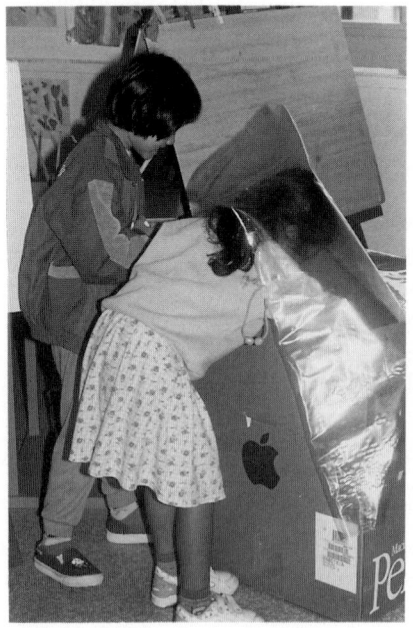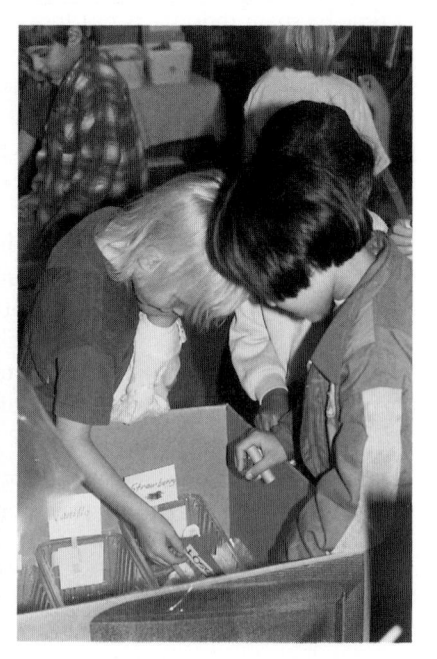

Plates 4.1 and 4.2 Only a cardboard box, a piece of plastic and some paper on sticks – but this 'freezer' was in constant use as these children selected their favourite iceblocks at the iceblock shop. (Photos courtesy of Northgate State Preschool.)

decisions. If, however, they can go to the storeroom and select any materials that they think can be affixed to their box, then they have many more choices and decisions to make. They also have opportunities to make predictions about what will or won't stick, as well as opportunities to test out their predictions.

Messages are also conveyed by the way in which time is used. Have you ever imagined what children must feel when they are told to pack away their intricate block building only minutes after they have completed it, and before they have had a chance to play with it? The space the block building is occupying may be needed for a group time so, in one sense, the request to pack away may be justified, but what message is this request sending? Is it saying, 'Your building and your concentrated efforts are not valued. Just pull down your building and stack the blocks away ... you can build another building to-morrow. To-day's building was of no great significance'? If your hard effort had been treated in a similar way on several occasions, would you build another building tomorrow? Children need lengthy periods of time in which to represent their ideas in some form and then to develop their play. The organization of the daily schedule needs to be such that it sends the message, 'There is plenty of time for you to develop your ideas and to play.'

In reflecting on their observations and experiences the students in the tutorial group agreed that, although they had noted ways of organizing the room and had thought a little about the effects of this organization on behaviour, they had not thought about physical organization in terms of the messages it sends. They also began to question *why* there was such a wide variation between settings, even for children of the same age, in the arrangement of space, the provision of materials and the use of time.

Examining reasons for particular organizational arrangements

Some students suggested that, while they recognized that organizational decisions influenced children's behaviour they had also noticed that, on some occasions, the reverse was true: the behaviour or needs of children in the group could affect a teacher's organizational decisions and actions. Ann, for instance, recalled how one of her supervising teachers moved the doll's house with its intricate and delicate furnishings into her office because the play had become too boisterous and some furniture had been broken when it was situated in the main activity room. All children were still welcome to play with the doll's house, but the smaller and quieter space afforded by the office meant that only small groups of children could be involved at the one time. Ann observed that, in the office setting, the play appeared to be more focused and less inhibited as the children took on the roles of the family figures they were holding. She thought this change in play may have stemmed from a greater sense of privacy. Ann said that when she shared her observations with her supervising teacher she had agreed, and had indicated that her decisions about the positioning of equipment were often influenced by observations of the children and the way in which particular settings seemed to affect their behaviour.

Other students suggested that the physical design of the building and playground, or even weather conditions, could influence the way in which the physical environment is organized. Joanne described a situation she had experienced on her last practicum which had brought home to her that weather and lack of space did affect the children's behaviour and level of activity, as well as her own. She said:

> We had two weeks of non-stop rain and both the children and I were beginning to go a little crazy ... and my patience was beginning to wear thin. One morning ... another wet one ... I was on the verandah talking to Rachel about her painting when I heard a group of children running inside. Without thinking I said, 'Don't run inside! You might slip and hurt yourselves.' That's when I realized I was beginning to say 'don't' and 'no' too often. After all, if I was 5 I would have wanted to run inside ... or anywhere! It was after that ... and a discussion with my supervising teacher ... that I decided to set up a mini-obstacle course indoors to compensate for the children's lack of physical activity outdoors. I also tried to avoid negative directions and use more positive comments when I could.

By thinking critically about the children's behaviour and her own responses Joanne was able to see that the confined space was impacting on the children's actions and her own. In proposing and trialling an alternative arrangement to overcome the impact, Joanne was, in fact, taking an important step in preparing to organize her own classroom.

Proposing alternative arrangements in particular situations

As a student teacher in your supervising teacher's setting there will be few opportunities for you to make or trial any major changes to the organization of the environment. Situations are likely to arise, however, as they did for Joanne, which will provide you with the chance to think and test out some alternative strategies and minor changes in arrangements. In the tutorial, Kellie recounted how she had realized that even little things, such as where she sat to read the story to the 3-year-olds, could influence their behaviour. Kellie had positioned herself so that the group was looking at some open shelves. She hadn't realized that the teacher had placed some very attractive puppets on those shelves just that morning. As Kellie was about to read the story one of the children, Sally, noticed the puppets, and, with an excitement that was contagious, immediately went and picked up the mouse puppet. Needless to say, that was the end of Kellie's planned story that day. After that experience, Kellie said she checked out what the children would be looking at before she positioned herself at group time, and, where possible, eliminated any distractions.

At the end of the tutorial, some students said they felt reasonably confident about planning and organizing the physical environment for learning and teaching. Others, however, said that while they were aware of some of the influencing factors, they often didn't realize what the effects of these factors might be. In other words, they had difficulty predicting what might happen. Because the ability to predict the 'possible trajectory of events in classrooms and the way specific actions affect situations' (Doyle, 1990: 355) is essential for effective teaching, it is important that you develop this skill. If you find predicting difficult, here are some actions you can take during your teaching practice which may help to improve your ability to predict:

- Select a particular incident (e.g., a child who refuses to come and sit with the group; a child who swears at you when you ask for the puzzles to be put away).
- Write down at least two alternative strategies you could use in that particular situation.
- Make yourself 'predict' the possible consequences of each of these strategies.
- Ask yourself to outline the message you think each particular strategy might convey to a child.
- Decide on your action and trial the chosen strategy at the next opportunity.
- Observe children's responses to your action, and consider whether or not their behaviour or response is consistent with the message you thought they would receive.
- If the children's response was not what you anticipated, try to work out the reasons why. If their response matched your prediction, give yourself a pat on the back ... then write down why you thought your action was successful!

Messages resulting from organizational decisions

In an effort to become more aware of the messages that can be conveyed by actions and decisions, the students in the tutorial group visited early childhood settings to look for the main message they felt teachers were conveying by their organization of the physical environment. (This may be something you could do if you are able to visit your centre prior to the practicum.) In looking for the message, the students considered not only the organization of space, resources and time but also the apparent effects of these on the children's responses and behaviour. The teachers who agreed to have students visit were aware that the students were looking for messages in their environment and were happy to talk with them at the conclusion of the visit.

Jodie, after her visit to a preschool for 4–5-year-old children, said that the teacher seemed to be conveying this message: 'Here is an environment that

invites and challenges you to use your initiative and resourcefulness.'
She presented her reasons for arriving at her conclusion this way:

When I first walked into the classroom before the session started I couldn't help noticing how different it looked from many of the other preschool rooms I have seen. It looked rather bare, with lots of empty spaces on the floor. The ceiling wasn't decorated with loads of bright coloured hanging 'things' but there were children's paintings displayed on the walls. The room still contained all the resources of any other preschool – puzzles, books in a corner with lots of comfy cushions, a writing corner and an area for easel painting. The other resources were arranged differently, however. There were large, hollow blocks stacked against one wall with the project blocks on two different trolleys in other parts of the room. The storeroom door was open and it was full of a great variety of recyclable material neatly organized in boxes. The collage trolley was easily accessible from both sides and close to a work bench. I was surprised at the numbers of sticky tape dispensers, staplers, and pairs of scissors that were provided.

Of particular interest to me was how the room changed from this quiet empty space before the children, as a group, had discussed their ideas for their play, to a hive of activity after the discussion, with children interacting with one another, with the teacher, and with all the resources in the room. The children took advantage of the space normally occupied by tables and chairs to create their own play areas. Having the different types of blocks spread around the room meant that many children, both boys and girls, had access to them and used them for many different purposes. Where the children chose to play was up to them, and problem solving occurred in many instances. For example, Jay wanted to build his house in the storeroom doorway, but how would people be able to get in and out of the storeroom? The children were challenged to think about everything, from where to play, to the types of resources they could use to make the wings of the plane, or to clean up the oil spill that was affecting the penguins. (This was a pretend game that some children had decided to play. Such a spill has been featuring in television news programs.)

I felt that it was not just the physical environment to which these children were responding. Sue, the teacher, had set up an environment where the children had access to stimulating, thought-provoking discussions which enabled the children to take the initiative and show resourcefulness. By organizing the room in a way which allowed the children to impose their own organization, the children also had freedom of expression and opportunities to explore materials as well as their ideas. It seemed that the children were learning through hands-on experiences, through making decisions, solving problems and learning to use their initiative. The most interesting aspect for me was that all the children's actions seemed purposeful and personally relevant.

When Jodie talked with Sue, the teacher, at the end of the session, she found that Sue had, in fact, written down the messages she was wanting to convey in her philosophy in *The Diary of a Preschool Teacher* (1985). This philosophy is expressed in terms of the type of environment Sue wants to provide for children. Jodie was unaware of this diary when she visited, and was interested to compare her own impressions with what Sue had written. These are some of the statements taken from Sue's introduction to her diary:

I want preschool to be a place where. . .

- Children can work in a 'real' climate – real in the sense that their ideas and thoughts may be constructively criticised but their efforts of doing and thinking will always be valued.
- Children's thinking and talking about their ideas is valued as much as the products and actions which can be seen.
- Children can use materials as tools in posing and solving problems.
- Children can develop their own style of pulling out the facts about the world rather than learning the facts about something.
- Children can work at their own pace and level of development so that they feel a sense of satisfaction and achievement.

Plate 4.3 As these children prepared to feed the animals in their wild-life park, they had the freedom to play with materials, with one another and their ideas. (Photo courtesy of Northgate State PreSchool.)

- Children can develop skills in a real way and for a real purpose. The need for these will inevitably arise through play.
- Children can have the freedom to play with materials, with each other, and with their thoughts and to re-create important events in their lives.

(Thomas, 1985:1)

What are your views concerning the match between Jodie's impressions and the kinds of messages and experiences Sue was hoping her environment would provide? For me, Jodie's description of the room arrangement seemed to illustrate clearly Sue's statements. For instance, the ways in which the room's organization encouraged children to impose some of their sense of order, to use a wide range of open-ended materials in creating their buildings and games, and to be actively involved in expressing their ideas, playing and making decisions, indicated that children were able to work in a 'real' environment which challenged them to use their initiative and resourcefulness.

LINKING BELIEFS ABOUT LEARNING AND TEACHING WITH ORGANIZATIONAL DECISIONS

If you think about Sue's statements, you can see that they are expressing her views about the kind of experiences that she believes will assist young children to learn. She has taken these beliefs and translated them into a picture of her 'ideal' environment for young children – what she wants children to experience in her preschool. I talked with Sue about how she arrived at this point in her thinking, and she said that it had taken many years of working with young children and many years of thinking about the nature of that work. Sue's experience may provide you with some pointers for developing your thinking about your 'ideal' environment.

As a *student teacher* Sue said she had:

- noted many different organizational arrangements;
- thought about what worked and what didn't work, and had tried, often unsuccessfully, to think about why;
- tested out her own ideas when given the opportunity;
- attempted to link her actions with her beliefs, but had found this very difficult because she wasn't sure about her beliefs!

As a *teacher* Sue said she had:

- tended, at first, to organize in ways similar to those used by 'respected' supervising teachers;
- gradually developed her own form of organization as she came to know the children and responded to their needs;

- looked at the environment from the children's perspectives as well as her own;
- begun to question familiar forms of organization and explore new forms (e.g., balancing time for different activities over a week instead of a day; leaving 'buildings' up so that play could be continued the next day);
- closely observed and analysed children's responses to new forms of organization;
- come to visualize ideals for children in terms of the types of learning environment she wanted them to experience.

After considering your own experiences, Sue's comments, and those made by the students in the tutorial, you will have realized that organizing the physical aspects of the environment is a far more complex task than it may at first appear. Not only are there all the dimensions of the use of space and time and the nature of resources and their presentation to think about, but there are also their possible effects and messages to consider. The organization of the physical environment is further complicated by the fact that, in early childhood settings, unplanned events can occur which change the nature and organization of that environment. For instance, paint can be spilt; a child can fall and need attention; there is an unexpected birthday celebration to fit in; or children can become so involved in an activity that the time schedule changes. Although you cannot control or prevent some of these 'happenings', you can recognize the need to be flexible and be prepared to adapt and change aspects of your organization.

BEING PREPARED

There is also another vital element relating to the organization of the physical environment that needs to be highlighted. This is the teacher's ability to be sufficiently prepared and organized to present activities and experiences in ways that challenge children's learning and thinking at appropriate moments. As a student teacher you must show that you are thoroughly prepared for any learning experiences that you present. You have to recognize that your own organization – or lack of it – also affects the smooth running of the classroom, as well as the children's behaviour.

Have you ever had that dreadful feeling of being totally disorganized? Most of us have! Our disorganized moments are generally memorable occasions, but memorable for the wrong reasons! Maria had such an experience during her last teaching practice with a Year One class, which she has agreed to share. She wrote in her journal:

> This afternoon was the last straw. I am just about ready to throw it all in! After the chaos of yesterday I thought the children might benefit from a 'fun' Friday afternoon activity. I had planned to read the book about bubbles and afterwards engage the children in a bubble-blowing activity. A simple enough plan ... but I hadn't taken into account a series of stuff–ups. First of all I was rostered on playground duty. I

was not aware of this until Mrs F, my supervising teacher, came to find out why I hadn't come out to do the duty. This was unfortunate because I had been planning to set up the equipment during this break. 'Well', I thought, 'it doesn't really matter. I will still have time to prepare when we return to class because Mrs F has to finish off the Maths lesson.'

Think again, Maria! When we returned to class Mrs F settled the children down, and I thought, 'Great! I'll go and set everything up now.' Instead, she told the children to go and get their hats because Miss T had a special activity planned for this afternoon. I nearly dropped dead! I looked at her and she must have read the look of panic on my face. I approached her feeling more and more anxious and confessed that I had nothing prepared yet. Oh! It was an absolute nightmare. Mrs F was not very impressed, and basically said, 'Well then, what are you going to do?'

I ended up running madly around from classroom to classroom trying to collect containers and then racing up to the staff room to make up the bubble mixture. This made me feel so embarrassed and humiliated. After a week of feeling pretty confident, I had landed flat on my face! Meanwhile, Mrs F was reading a story while the children waited for me.

I finally returned to class and rushed through explaining what we were going to do. We were running out of time and I didn't even think to mention safety or behaviour expectations. My only thoughts were on getting through this experience. We got outside and I thought, 'OK, everything's fine now.' Was I wrong! From the moment we made it into the adventure playground, chaos reigned supreme. The children were running around and wouldn't listen to my instructions. They were climbing on equipment and fighting over the containers. I tried to implement calming strategies – hands on heads, clapping rhythms, but they would not pay me any attention. Tahlia got some of the bubble mixture in her eye and Dominic tripped while running around chasing bubbles. By this stage I was a nervous wreck and nearly out of my mind with despair. I couldn't control the children and Mrs F was standing over near the fence, watching, but not becoming involved in my 'fun' afternoon. Finally she walked over to me, and the children reverted to their normally sedate behaviour. By now the thought of someone else being in charge had me almost weeping with relief.

Discussing the afternoon's events later with Mrs F helped me somewhat, but as I write this story now I feel so utterly stupid. I recognize that it was a good learning experience, and I will endeavour never to repeat this mistake, but the event has diminished my early confidence, and, as I am expected to take whole days in the next two weeks, I feel more nervous than I had thought I would.

At the end of her teaching practice, some weeks later, Maria reflected on her experience this way:

To many this story might seem meaningless – you made a mistake,

Maria – get over it. But for me, it was a crisis point affecting my confidence in my ability in becoming a teacher. I can so vividly recall my feelings of frustration and helplessness as the children completely ignored my requests to settle down. At the time I recall thinking, 'What is wrong with these children? What a terrible, horrible bunch of children!' Looking back it would have been so easy to just blame them and justify the whole experience by pretending that these children had no self-control and were complete and utter ratbags. Had I done that I would have learned nothing and I really would have been a failure. Instead I chose to grasp this opportunity and benefit from it ... to give myself a chance to really learn something about teaching.

I believe the absolute chaos stemmed from my lack of organization and preparation. This neglect, in turn, led to feelings of anger, confusion and failure, emotions which generated further *Angst* as the children intuitively picked up on my feelings of inadequacy and frustration. By the time I got home that afternoon I was ready to throw it all in. A chat with a teacher friend of mine over that weekend helped to change my perspective. She called it a learning experience, and reminded me that the ultimate failure would be not to learn something about the value of organization and preparation.

If I were to be faced with the same situation again, I would immediately terminate the activity so as to avoid any further accidents and return the children to the classroom. It is not advisable to take a group of twenty-five Year One children into an adventure playground, give them bubble-blowing equipment and *then* try to explain safety rules and behavioural expectations. These should be made very clear beforehand. While my first mistake was being unprepared, and my second was to fail to explain any safety or behaviour rules, my third mistake was to lose all control and confidence in my role as a teacher. By remaining relaxed, calm and confident in manner it is easier to take hold of a situation and diffuse it, rather than let it continue to gain momentum and eventually reach crisis point.

Maria has told her story so clearly, I'm sure you will be able to learn from it too. For me, Maria's story exemplifies how events can intertwine and snowball in classroom situations. It demonstrates how what appears to be an insignificant oversight can turn into chaos! For instance, Maria's lack of organization in not having the bubble activity prepared led to a personal sense of inadequacy and rush – which in turn meant expectations were not made clear to children – which resulted in over-excited and out-of-control behaviour – which reinforced Maria's feeling of inadequacy – which children sensed and played on – which in turn led to chaos!

Maria's story also illustrates how closely interwoven the social and physical aspects of the environment are, with the lack of physical organization resulting in the breakdown of the social organization of the class. It is vital, then, that in thinking about the creation of learning environments you also consider the social aspects that contribute to the learning process.

PROMOTING A SUPPORTIVE SOCIAL ENVIRONMENT

Textbooks on early childhood teaching stress the importance of the provision of emotionally warm and supportive environments. Children need to feel accepted and secure, to have a trusting relationship with adults and a developing sense of confidence in themselves as being capable and competent if they are to learn effectively. Just as the physical organization of the classroom sends messages to children about what they are expected to do and how they are to do it, so, too, the social climate of the classroom sends messages to children about who they are, how they are valued and what they are capable of doing and being.

As you become familiar with your teaching practice situation you will quickly sense whether the environment is a warm and caring one with a happy, busy hum about it, or whether the environment is cold and impersonal, a place where children seem to wander or look bored, and be tearful or argumentative. While it is easy to gain these general impressions, it is often harder to pinpoint what factors are contributing to the creation of particular social and emotional climates in classrooms. It is important that you try to do so, however, as this knowledge will help you establish a caring and supportive environment in your early childhood setting. You need to find answers to this question:

• What are the key elements that contribute to a caring and supportive environment?

A number of students, in thinking about their responses to this question, recounted personal experiences from their own school-days or observations from teaching practice experiences which, for them, highlighted particular aspects which contributed to, or in some cases, worked against the creation of supportive and caring environments. By looking beyond the descriptive level of their accounts you can discover some of the more subtle yet powerful ways teachers demonstrate support, or lack of it, to children. For these student teachers the ways teachers offered or failed to offer support related to:

• valuing children's contributions and building self-esteem;
• welcoming and celebrating cultural diversity;
• providing meaningful contexts for learning;
• fostering a sense of independence and responsibility in children;
• engendering a sense of fairness.

As you think about these students' experiences and your own memories that will be sparked by them, you will no doubt identify many other ways whereby you can show children that you value and respect them and want to support them in their learning.

Valuing children's contributions and building self-esteem

If you think back to your own school-days, I'm sure you will recall an incident which left you with the impression that you were misunderstood, or that you were being misjudged or treated unfairly. Allan, a final year student, recalled such an incident as he thought about some of the factors that were influencing his own approach to teaching, and why he felt so strongly that all children deserved respect. He wrote:

> If there was one incident from my own schooling which has helped to shape my philosophy and approach to teaching, it is what happened to me in Year Two. My teacher, Mrs K, was quite a good teacher who made learning fun for us. I was a very bright and inquisitive child and I was nearly always first to put my hand up in order to ask or answer a question. Mrs K got to know that I knew the answers and asked the others instead of me. Even when I wanted to ask questions Mrs K would say, 'Put your hand down, Allan. You know the answer, now stop being silly.' This type of treatment continued until the day of our maths exam, when I fell from grace. The question which I remember most vividly was on measurement. It was, 'How many feet tall are you?' I had no concept of the linear measurement so I looked at the size of my foot and proceeded to approximate just how many feet tall I thought I was. I came up with thirteen and wrote it down. The teacher laughed as she read my answer out to the whole class. The other children laughed too and I cried. The one positive to come from this experience was that Mrs K started to ask me to answer questions again.
>
> Although it was a very traumatic experience for me at the time, I now see it as a very valuable one as I develop my thinking about teaching. I continually reflect on my teaching practices and interactions with children in an attempt to ensure that I provide a warm and supportive environment which encourages explorations and approximation.

Allan's story highlights the importance of valuing each child's contribution and appreciating the nature of the thinking that underlies it. There is no place whatever for ridiculing or making fun of a child's effort. Such actions indicate a total lack of respect for the person concerned and work against the development of self-confidence and self-esteem. Teachers' actions must send the message that each child's effort and contribution is valued even if they do not result in the 'right' answer, and that it is natural that when we do our own thinking we will sometimes make mistakes.

Welcoming and celebrating cultural diversity

Gail's teaching practice experience in a Year One class of 5–6-year-olds had a major impact on her views about the importance of respecting and valuing cultural diversity. She wrote:

> After my first day I was very aware of Ahmud. He was a child who 'stood out.' He was 6 years old and the oldest of four children. The family had recently arrived from Somalia and only the father had any grasp of English. There was little contact between the school and Ahmud's parents because of the language barrier, and no attempt was made by the school to break this barrier through using an interpreter service. I was told that on his first day at school Ahmud was handed a pair of scissors in order to cut. He held them and shrugged his shoulders. He did not know what they were, and, because he knew no English he didn't know how to ask about their use. No one, it seems, thought to demonstrate how scissors could be used.
>
> For the month I was in Ahmud's class as a student teacher I saw him fight daily battles . . . and lose. From my perspective Ahmud learned:
>
> - that if he was given instructions in English and didn't obey them he was sat on a chair away from the group;
> - to colour in endlessly during the school day because he wasn't considered capable of doing much more;
> - if an older child teased him in the playground and he hit that child, then he was sent to the principal and punished;
> - to DISLIKE school.
>
> Sadly, I observed first hand what happens when a child's needs are not considered, when the classroom is not looked at through the child's eyes, and a child's language and culture are not respected. I saw a child who cringed when his name was called; a child who sat and ate his lunch alone because no other child would be his friend. My heart ached for Ahmud, and I tried to show I cared and talked to him when I could. Even after a short time in school, however, Ahmud was so angry and confused that he had difficulty responding positively on the few occasions I was able to give him support. The memory of Ahmud's frustration will haunt me, but it will also ensure that I will make every effort to show that I respect all children and that cultural diversity is to be valued. I want all the children to know that it is a privilege to have a child who speaks another language in the class . . . and that it is a privilege to have such children as friends.

Gail's observation of Ahmud's experience highlights not only the teacher's failure to intervene positively to assist Ahmud to maintain his confidence and self-esteem, but also her failure to acknowledge and value diversity. Her total lack of respect for another culture and language was evident in her actions and was sending all the wrong messages, not only to Ahmud, but to all the other children in the class. Gail's experience highlights the importance of developing strategies which show children what can be gained when all cultures and languages are valued and respected. Some books that may help you develop these strategies include Derman-Sparks and the ABC Task Force (1989) and Creaser and Dau (1996).

Providing meaningful contexts for learning

Rachel quickly became aware that the children in the Year One class where she was undertaking teaching practice lacked a sense of enthusiasm and excitement about learning. She was upset to hear Year One children say that school was boring. In trying to pinpoint reasons why the children were not excited about learning and the wonderful world of literacy that was gradually opening up for them, Rachel felt that the children's own experiences were not being considered and that they were being asked to learn in contexts that had little meaning or relevance to them. Rachel decided to plan some experiences that would encourage the children to read and write for personally meaningful reasons. She described her efforts this way:

> The children were just beginning story writing. The teacher would select a topic (usually something to do with the current class reader) and everybody would attempt to do some writing on this topic. I negotiated with my teacher to plan some story writing where the children could select their own topic. My teacher told me she thought this wouldn't work 'because children this age need a lot of structure', but she said I needed to find this out for myself!
>
> To begin the experience I explained that we would be selecting our own topic for writing. I modelled selecting a topic. I said I was going to write about an activity we had done in class that morning and showed them how this could be done. After discussing some writing and spelling strategies, the children went to their places to write their own stories. Within a few minutes the children were saying, 'I don't know what to write about.' The few children who had written anything had copied my sentence word for word. The experience was a disaster. I had trouble controlling the group as the children swarmed around me asking, 'What are we doing?' The experience met none of my objectives and had to be abandoned so that I could regain the attention of the class. I felt such a failure. I had proved my teacher right!
>
> I went home and reflected on the experience. I realized that the children were used to being told what to do and following instructions. When I gave them freedom to select their own topic it was a totally unfamiliar situation and they genuinely didn't know what to do. I wanted to plan another writing experience and apply what I had learned but I knew I would have to find a suitable opportunity. A few days later, after a night of heavy rain, Ashley stood up in the discussion time and began talking with much excitement about how there was a flood

at her house, and a black-out, and how they couldn't cook dinner. Soon the whole group was buzzing with discussion about fallen trees, flooded bridges, sad wet dogs, take-away pizzas, and candle lights. I could see this was the perfect opportunity for the children to write about something that was personally interesting. They had a reason for writing about and drawing their own experiences. They could tell others about what happened at their house.

The children really extended themselves in the writing as they tried to convey meaning. I was delighted with the oral communications as children shared their writing and experiences with one another in small groups. Even my supervising teacher was impressed with many of the children's attempts. Through this experience I learned that children in a very teacher-directed environment need to be gradually and thoughtfully introduced to a more autonomous style of learning. I found that children did put more effort into writing when the topic was of personal interest or meaning and that I had fewer problems maintaining control when children understood what was expected of them. My belief that it is important that children see a reason and purpose in their learning was strengthened.

It is interesting to think about the messages children were getting from Rachel's actions which stemmed from her belief in the importance of purposeful learning. By seeking to find topics that were of interest to children, Rachel was communicating the message that she valued and respected the children's own experience and ideas, and that she was interested in what interested them. As well, the children were able to experience the respect of other children as they came together to share their personal accounts of an event that had affected them all. In an indirect way Rachel was also dealing with the children's negative feelings about school by enabling them to experience more relevant and interesting learning activities.

Fostering a sense of independence and responsibility in children

There are many ways in which teachers send messages to children that they are competent and capable. By encouraging the under 5s to develop self-help skills so that they can dress, feed and toilet themselves, for example, a teacher is showing respect, not only for a child's ability and competence, but also for their right to feel independent and responsible when this is appropriate. The ways in which routines such as morning tea and lunch, tidy-up and rest times are handled in your teaching practice situations can also provide you with many insights concerning the amount of respect paid to children. For instance, when preparing to make the transition between playtime and lunch, are children given some notice that it will soon be time to finish their game or activity? This allows them to bring some 'closure' to their play, and, in a subtle way, gives the message that their activity is valued. When making the transition, are the children lined up and kept waiting with nothing to do, or are children able to contribute and take some responsibility for tidying the setting before moving independently to the next activity? Is sufficient time allowed for nappy changing and toileting toddlers so that they are unhurried and can delight in warm interactions with adults who respond to their babbles and engage in peek-a-boo games? These leisurely, caring interactions all help to build a child's sense of being valued and respected.

Kylie was distressed by the way in which rest time was handled in one of her preschool teaching practice settings. She wrote:

> No matter how frustrating or difficult a child is, no adult has the right to 'pin' a child to their bed. Surely there must be better strategies ... giving a child a book, for example. Do all the children need to be doing exactly the same thing at one time ... lying like statues on their stretchers for one hour? Do they all need to be covered by their sheet? At any other time of the day the teacher encourages individual children to make choices. What is so different about rest time? Why does it need to be so regimented? I tired of listening to my nagging voice – 'sheet bags under your beds', 'lie straight on your bed', 'shut your eyes'.

Bed ideas – to help us rest

Figure 4.1 The children's rules for rest time

97

Perhaps I was particularly distressed by this situation because seventeen years ago I was one of those 'wrigglers and disrupters' during rest time. I distinctly remember my stretcher being placed under the keyboard of the piano so I could not move my stretcher about or sit up without bumping my head. Although I believe that some routines are important in order for children to feel secure, unnecessary control will cause continual pressure on both the children and staff. To me it seems just as important to respect the individual needs of children during routine times such as lunch and rest as it does at other times of the day.

Rosanda had a much more positive experience of rest time during her preschool teaching practice. At her centre, after a short period of quiet rest, children were able to have drawing boards on which to draw while they rested. One day, however, a number of children were restless in spite of having their drawing boards. Rosanda described what happened in her journal:

> After observing that the children were having difficulty settling (it had been a very exciting morning with a visit from a theatre group), the teacher said that there really seemed a problem at rest time today and she would need everyone's help to solve it. This group just love dealing with problems and they quickly came together to discuss some ideas. The children decided they needed some rules and came up with several. The teacher wrote down the rules and the children illustrated them.

What different messages children in these two settings were receiving. In Kylie's preschool, children were expected to conform to a certain standard of behaviour, set and controlled by the adults with no allowance being made for individual differences or needs. In contrast, in Rosanda's preschool, the teacher was sensitive and responsive to children's needs and involved them in setting reasonable limits. This enabled children to experience self-control and to participate in a shared responsibility.

Engendering a sense of fairness

Ruth undertook a teaching practice in a preschool where her supervising teacher was keen to promote respect for the rights of others. Her teacher regarded the notion of social justice as being equated with fairness (Sebastian-Nickell and Milne, 1992). She wanted children to treat one another fairly, to value difference and diversity, to respect the rights of others and to be able to resolve conflict in a fair way. Ruth observed many discussions which occurred during play where children were challenged to think about what would be fair. She detailed one of these discussions in her journal:

> Two groups of children had built their houses from large hollow blocks and pieces of cardboard, side by side in the middle of the room. They

had been quite amicable neighbours until Karen picked up Charlie, the favourite toy dog, from a nearby shelf and claimed that Charlie lived at her house. Jane, who lived in the other house, immediately disputed this and said that Charlie lived in her house. The teacher listened to the argument from a distance, but, seeing that feelings were running high and that the argument was not going to resolve itself, came over and said, 'What can we do about Charlie? We've only got one dog and two households that want him?'

KAREN We could make another one.

JANE And we'll have the real Charlie.

TEACHER Well, what do you think? Would that be fair? (*Neither Karen nor Jane thought it would, so the teacher asked them again what they could do.*)

JANE We could share him.

TEACHER How will you do that?

JANE We could join our houses together.

KAREN Yeah! You could live with me and I could live with you.

JANE You come to live with me first.

KAREN No! I'm not going to live in your house first.

TEACHER Oh dear! What are you going to do?

JANE We could both be mothers.

KAREN We could sleep together. . . in bunks.

JANE And if we have two dogs one could sleep on the top bunk and the other on the bottom bunk.

TEACHER But you've only got one dog.

KAREN You could have a ring-tailed possum. My sister goes out at night looking for a ring-tailed possum.

JANE No, I want Charlie.

At this stage the teacher suggested they go to the storeroom to see how they could make their beds. They came back with cushions, large pieces of material and a small mattress, and made their beds with Karen still clutching Charlie under her arm. As they got into bed, however, Charlie was placed between them, and, as the play developed, Charlie was forgotten as they had to care for their very sick daughter.

Many discussions like this one seemed to occur during the children's play. There would be real conflict but there would also be talking about how the problem could be overcome. I realized that the way in which the teacher intervened enabled the children to do most of the problem solving for themselves, although the teacher did keep bringing them back to think about whether what they were suggesting would be fair.

In this preschool, the teacher was sending a clear message that if there was a problem, then children were capable of solving it in a fair way. In order to do this, however, children had to listen to and consider other people's suggestions for solving the problem and to think about whether the suggested solution was a fair one. The teacher supported them in this task.

It is interesting to think about the underlying messages that were flowing to children from the teachers' and student teachers' actions presented in these examples. Were their actions saying to children, 'I value your ideas, and effort – your different language and culture. I respect your ability to make decisions and choices – to be independent when it is safe to be. I trust you to take some responsibility and to consider and care about the rights of others'? Or were their actions saying the reverse? Given that the memories of such actions and messages were still vivid for Allan and Kylie so many years later, it would seem very important to begin to clarify the types of messages you want to convey by your actions and decisions if you are to provide a supportive social and emotional climate for children's learning.

SUMMARY

The discussion in this chapter has focused on the physical as well as the social and emotional factors that are seen to contribute to effective learning–teaching environments. A number of steps for building your understanding of these factors and their effects have been suggested. These include:

- noting similarities and differences in how early childhood settings are designed and organized in terms of space, materials and time;
- considering possible reasons for particular organizational decisions;
- becoming aware of the messages conveyed to children by organizational decisions and teachers' actions;
- observing the ways in which the behaviour of children and teachers is influenced by organizational factors;
- developing an ability to predict children's responses to particular organizational decisions and consequent messages;
- evaluating the physical and social aspects of the setting in the light of your beliefs about learning and teaching.

Although there are few opportunities for you to make or trial major organizational changes because schedules, routines and room arrangements are generally established when teaching practice is undertaken, there will be opportunities to assess your own organizational and decision-making skills as you fulfil some of your teaching practice requirements, for example:

- when planning and taking an activity with children;
- when settling and taking a larger group for a lesson, story or music session;
- when assisting children to make a transition from one activity to another;
- when in control for a certain period of the day;
- when assisting in resolving a conflict situation;
- when helping children to act on their ideas.

It is important that you are frank and honest in your appraisal of your own efforts as you reflect on such situations. Ask yourself some questions: Did I explain my expectations clearly? Were the children able to contribute to the decision making? Did they understand the reason for the request? Was the experience an interesting and enjoyable one and why was this? If it did not hold the children's interest, what were reasons for this? What could I do to improve the experience?

Ask your supervising teacher, too, for suggestions as to how you could have prevented difficulties arising or for some alternative strategies that you could have used. It is important to acknowledge the problems you may experience as you develop your organizational abilities and learn from your mistakes. By talking or writing honestly of your experience and seeking reasons for its success or otherwise you are able to develop and refine your strategies and abilities.

SUGGESTED ACTIVITIES

- Design and sketch your 'ideal' physical environment for a particular age group (for example, babies – 3-year-olds; 3–5-year-olds; 5–8-year-olds). Indicate some of the design features, such as natural lighting, landscaping and fixed equipment. Show how you would arrange your selected indoor and outdoor furniture and equipment and how you would store materials. Be prepared to discuss the reasons for your design and choice of resources.

- Give examples of the use of space and equipment, the selection and storage of materials, and the daily schedule that you have observed. Outline the messages you felt were being conveyed to children by these particular forms of organization and explain how the organization was contributing to these messages.

- How would you organize transitions in order to send the message that you want children to be as independent as possible and that you trust them to take some reponsibility for their actions? Outline some specific actions you would take.

- What recyclable materials would you want in your storeroom for the under 3s; 3–5-year-olds; 5–8-year olds? Where would you get these supplies and how would you store them? What are some of the best storage ideas you have seen?

- If you believe that it is important for children to have opportunities to make choices, how would you organize your environment to maximize choice? List and describe at least five things you would do.

- Describe five actions you would take as a teacher to ensure that children feel they are in an emotionally safe and supportive environment. Discuss these actions with a friend and outline why you feel they are important. Also list five things you would 'never do' and give your reasons.

- Think about where you would prefer to be – in a suburban shopping centre or walking through a national park. What are the features of your preferred environment which attract you? In thinking about the reasons for your own preferred environment, draw some implications for the planning of environments for children.

5

DEVELOPING A PRACTICAL THEORY AND PRACTICAL SKILLS

In this chapter we are thinking about how you can extend your understanding of teaching young children and further develop your practical skills. This will be done by:

- considering how you can develop your practical theory of teaching;
- highlighting strategies for developing practical skills;
- examining how your practical theory can help you to refine your practical skills.

DEVELOPING A PRACTICAL THEORY: WHY AND HOW?

An important aspect of becoming a teacher is to develop your own theory of teaching. Although this may sound a difficult thing to do, you are more than likely developing your own theory without even being aware that you are! Whenever you talk with friends about teaching, reflect on your own experiences of school, undertake readings and assignments and think about your observations and experiences of teaching, you are, in fact, building your own personal construct of what teaching is for you at that particular time. If you have shared your ideas about teaching with friends, you have probably discovered that your 'theories' vary from those of others. This is because you have not only had different personal experiences, but your thoughts about teaching and your perceptions of your experiences will have been influenced by your particular beliefs and values.

Developing your own theory of teaching is important, because it serves as a background against which you make decisions about the practical actions you can take. In fact, Handal and Lauvås (1987: 9) argue that it should be termed a 'practical theory' because it is 'the strongest determining factor in [a teacher's] educational practice'. It influences not only what you do but how you do it. It is important, then, that in developing your practical theory you develop your knowledge, not only of *what* teaching is, but also of *how* teaching can be undertaken.

Don't feel too concerned if, at this stage, you can't write or even talk about your practical theory in any coherent way. Even experienced teachers have difficulty doing this. What you need to do, as a student teacher, is to become more conscious of your thinking about teaching, as this is fundamental to the development of your practical theory. You can develop your awareness of the nature of teaching in a number of ways during teaching practice. Here are some suggestions:

- Describe situations and ask questions about the teaching actions of your supervising teacher and yourself.
- Explore the reasons as to why you feel particular learning – teaching experiences were successful or otherwise.
- Be prepared to challenge and extend your existing knowledge about teaching.
- Consider ethical issues associated with teaching.

Describing situations and asking questions about teaching actions

From your very first visit to an early childhood setting it is important that you try to form a picture in your own mind of what is happening. Such a setting can seem confusing at first, with children and teachers continually on the move and engaging in a wide variety of activities. One starting point for building this picture is to write brief descriptions of particular situations. As you write these descriptions you will probably begin to ask questions about the teacher's actions and interactions with children. If you are able to participate and interact with children you can also ask questions about your own actions. The 'what', 'how', 'where', 'when' and 'why' type questions always provide useful prompts. At first you may find that you are focusing on the 'what' question. If you are writing descriptions of what the teacher did, or what you did and how the children responded, it is also interesting to add the 'why' question. Why did the teacher act in a particular way, or why did the children respond in the way they did? These descriptions and questions will help you, not only to become more aware of what is happening, but also of what is likely to happen if you do certain things in a certain way. This awareness develops your ability to anticipate and predict, which is a fundamental aspect of your practical theory.

Tammy made progress in building her practical theory during her last teaching practice, when she looked closely at what her supervising teacher did when preparing and presenting a lesson and compared these observations with her own approach. Tammy wrote:

> During this prac in a Year One class I focused on what the teacher did. I noticed that the teacher seemed to have so many resources and ideas to draw on and I basically had nothing. I had many a discussion with my teacher about this and she had many a comment to make. Her main

concern was that I seemed ill-prepared in the management part of teaching. And honestly I could see her point. During the first week of prac, before this discussion, I hadn't thought about the resources that were vital when I planned the experiences. They were such little things, like having a pen ready when I was about to mark the roll . . . or making sure there were enough crayons and scissors available for everyone . . . having a box of tissues within easy reach . . . and making sure that I knew where the book was that I planned to read. The list went on and on and, as I started to consider all the little things, my stomach sank. What type of teacher would I be if a great deal of the valuable learning time was lost due to my incompetence?

From then on I wrote every single resource down on my plan . . . from the scissors needed . . . to the glue for sticking the parts of the plant on to the poster. To my surprise these new plans ran like clockwork. Even though it took a little more organizing in the morning, I had everything there. When I have my own classroom it will be my responsibility to provide these resources and to know where everything is.

By asking herself why the teacher's lessons seemed to flow so much more smoothly than her own, Tammy discovered the value of preparation and organization. This became an important aspect of Tammy's practical theory at this stage in her understanding of teaching. Another student, Jenny, also began to ask questions about her own teaching actions in her very first teaching practice experience. She wrote:

When I entered this course in teacher education I had very little idea of what a teacher did. During my first teaching practice I fell in love with the notion of being a leader in a group of 3–4-year-old children who all willingly built me tall towers out of blocks, painted me a picture of their favourite thing, brought me flowers and looked cute in the dress-up clothes. The first activity I planned was balloon painting, because we had to plan and present an art activity as part of the teaching practice requirements. Although this was a lot of fun, I found it frustrating to see a child being told what to do in order to 'succeed' in this activity. I continued to carry out my set, planned activities, but I began to wonder what exactly teaching was. What was I doing when I sang a song with Lisa in time to her rhythm as she learned to push herself on the swing . . . or went and got the hose when I saw that David and Luke had built a dam in the sandpit? Were just my planned set activities teaching – or were these spontaneous actions based on my observations part of teaching too?

Even at this early stage in her experience, Jenny was beginning to identify some of her own values; namely, her preference for a child's own creative expression rather than conformity to an adult's view of success. She was also trying to figure out in her own mind what teaching is. Does teaching mean making the most of each moment – the planned and the unplanned? Can the unplanned, spontaneous responses or activities which result from a teacher's observation be regarded as teaching? These questions were also very important ones for Jenny in developing her practical theory. She needed to go further, however, and find answers to them. This is not an easy task. One way to approach it, though, is to consider the effects of these spontaneous actions on children. If you can see that children's experiences are being enriched and thinking challenged by such responses, it seems reasonable to regard these actions as an important part of teaching.

Clarifying reasons for particular responses

Exploring the reasons as to why particular learning experiences appear successful or otherwise is another useful means of building your practical theory. Graham found it helpful to think about why an experience which had begun in rather difficult circumstances worked so well. He wrote in his journal:

> I had just set up the obstacle course outside this morning when it began to rain and I had to rush and bring the equipment on to the patio. Mrs G said we would still break up into our small groups, and, as I was to take the children at the obstacle course, I wasn't sure what to do. My eight children arrived on the patio and there I was with my jumble of boards, hoops, tunnel, trestles, mats, rope and balance beam. I told the children what had happened and suggested that they could help set up the obstacle course. They had some great ideas ... so many that they all wanted to talk at once. After we worked out that they each would be able to make a suggestion, we soon had a terrific 'course' with more obstacles than I had set. They worked out that they would need the mats under the higher boards 'so they wouldn't get hurt'. Some of the children who had difficulty explaining their ideas verbally were able to show the group what they meant by arranging the items themselves. Some of the ideas seemed rather dangerous so we talked about these and considered what might happen if.... The children were able to see and talk about the reasons for the concern and suggest some safe solutions. We spent so long setting up the course that the next group arrived for their turn after the children had only had one turn.
>
> The second group was not nearly as interested in overcoming the obstacles as the first group had been. Observing the lesser involvment of the second group compared with the enthusiasm of the first group made me realize just how important it is for children to have some say in what they do and how they do it. I also realized that, in setting up the course, the children were talking with each other, solving problems,

and seeing something come from their ideas. I think they learned far more than they would have done if it hadn't rained!

In describing what had happened, Graham was able to identify the features of the experience which in his view provided worthwhile learning. His experience with the second group provided him with a basis for comparison in terms of children's responses, and enabled him to think about why there was such a difference in the degree of involvment. When I talked with Graham about this experience he indicated that, whenever possible in the future, he would try to empower children by encouraging them to express and share their ideas for what they could do. He also said that he had realized just how much the way a teacher does things affects the number and nature of the learning opportunities children have. It is this type of thinking which leads you to incorporate certain types of actions into your practical theory.

Miranda discovered the value of clarifying the reasons why things can go wrong. She described her discoveries this way:

> I felt confident entering the book area to prepare for the story. The children responded immediately to my initial attempt at seeking attention when I sang 'Hello everybody'. It was straight after this that the problems began. Cameron got up and wandered over to the book-shelf and picked up a book. When I asked him to come back and sit down he ignored me. I decided to ignore him, but, just as I started to introduce the story Samantha jumped up and said she wanted to do a puzzle. (I guess she thought if Cameron could get away with it she could too.) By the time I'd talked Samantha into sitting down, all the other children were restless. Even when I began the story I never really regained their attention. As I read the story, I realized that it wasn't all that interesting. I kept stopping and reminding different children to 'tuck up their legs' and 'keep their hands to themselves', but while I did this the other children totally lost interest and also became fidgety. A couple of times I just put the book down and waited for them to be quiet, but this had no effect either.
>
> I hadn't dreamt this would happen so I hadn't prepared any strategies to deal with this situation. There I was in front of a group of preschoolers trying to make sense out of nothing! Interestingly, I didn't become frustrated. If I had, I might have been more direct with the children who needed it. So here I am writing an evaluation of a group time I hadn't sufficiently planned ... a major blunder! After a long discussion with my supervising teacher, who witnessed the whole disaster, I've come up with these ideas:
>
> • establish my leadership role right from the beginning;
> • settle the children and gain their attention with a song or clapping game;

- avoid pauses;
- state expectations clearly and expect responses;
- limit all possible distractions before beginning the story;
- if the story is not holding the children's interest be prepared to shorten it, or tell it in another way – by discussing pictures;
- if a child doesn't respond to a request, give a warning which contains a choice – 'If you are not going to sit on the mat with us and listen to the story you will have to sit on the chair near Mrs J's office. What are you going to choose to do?' If the child does not choose to sit with the group I must follow through on the consequence.

In thinking about the reasons for her lack of control, Miranda was able to clarify how she could have handled the situation more effectively. Thinking about the *how* of teaching is an important part of developing your practical theory. Knowing how to do something, however, doesn't necessarily mean that you are able to do it. You have to *use* that 'how to' knowledge in order to develop your practical skills. Miranda had a chance to do that the next time she took the group for a story.

> Following last week's disaster I very tentatively entered the story area today. I mentally went through the strategies I might need to use during the session and sat down. The initial settling period went smoothly and I only needed to speak to Kia and Jay about remembering what they needed to do during storytime. The story about a teddy bear was one that I knew would interest the children after our teddy bears' picnic, so it was relatively easy to maintain their interest. I put a lot of effort into the reading of it and involved the children in parts if their attention started to stray. I avoided long pauses and getting caught up talking to individual children. The children seemed to see me as being in control today, perhaps because I felt that I was.

Miranda's experience is a great example of the practical skills that can be developed if you are prepared to build your own practical theory by thinking about why a situation was not successful and identifying alternative strategies that are likely to be more successful. Although Miranda had read about group management skills and watched her supervising teacher manage the group, it was only after she experienced the situation herself that this previous knowledge began to be 'personalized' and incorporated into her own practical theory. To be a skilful teacher you have to be a thinking teacher. You also have to show that you can put your 'how to' knowledge into practice.

Being prepared to challenge and extend your existing knowledge about teaching

Accepting that your existing knowledge about teaching is subject to challenge and possible change is one of the most difficult aspects of building your practical theory. It is also what gives your practical theory a dynamic and creative form. Challenging or extending your teaching knowledge requires you to search continually for new meanings and understandings, consider them in the light of your existing knowledge and, perhaps, be prepared to change your views. For example, just as you feel you have come to understand what it means for children to 'learn through play', you may see a different teaching approach which presents some new ideas about the meaning of that term. Are you willing to think about these new ideas and perhaps incorporate them into your practical theory, or are you going to say, 'No! I've just found out what learning through play means and I'm not prepared to consider any new notions about play at this stage'? This is a decision you have to make and there may be circumstances where you need to consolidate your thinking before taking on board some different ideas. Be aware, though, that if you frequently decide that you need to consolidate, and ignore new information, you are in danger of having one teaching practice five times over rather than experiencing and benefiting from five teaching practices.

In an assignment focusing on play, Rhyll's reflections show how she was prepared to have her thinking challenged as she sought to understand 'play'. She wrote:

> I continue to search for answers to the question, 'Why is play so important to young children?' In seeking answers I was first confronted with the problem of what I meant by play. In an earlier assignment I defined play in terms of activities done for the enjoyment they give. I feel I have created a more complex picture of play since then. I now think of it as behaviour that has a number of characteristics. Play is intrinsically motivated, is free from externally imposed rules, has an 'as if' or pretend element, focuses on the means rather than the ends, and is controlled by the players who are actively involved (Rubin *et al.*, 1983). These characteristics provide me with a very different picture of play from the so-called play activities which teachers provide and expect children to undertake. I have seen these characteristics most in children's pretend play.
>
> During my last teaching practice in a preschool I was with a teacher who encouraged pretend play. I was fascinated by what I saw and heard. I recorded this conversation as Tim and Mike were preparing to go 'scuba diving'. Tim had finished making his air tank and was waiting for Mike to finish his. The teacher was helping Mike in this task.

TIM to MIKE   I might do a drawing while I'm waiting. (*He gets crayons and draws lines all over his paper.*)

TEACHER to TIM and MIKE   I wonder what the weather will be like for scuba diving?

TIM to TEACHER   I know what the weather's like 'cos I'm drawing what the weather map's like.

TEACHER to TIM (*looking at map*) Goodness, that looks like bad weather.

(*Tim keeps on drawing.*)

TEACHER to TIM   What does the weather map tell us?

TIM to TEACHER   Just look at it and you'll see.

TEACHER to TIM   It looks as though it will be a wild, rough sea. I don't think it will be safe enough to go down.

MIKE to TEACHER   We'll just stay in the water by the shore.

TEACHER to TIM and MIKE   Are you going to stay in the shallow part?

TIM to TEACHER   Yes – and then we'll go round to the deep part.

TEACHER to TIM and MIKE   Well look, the water currents are going this way. (*She draws arrows in a circle on Tim's drawing.*) They're going around and around and they're making the water very rough.

TIM to MIKE and TEACHER   O-Oh! It's going to be a whirlpool and we'll go here. (*He marks a spot in the circle on the map.*) Right there.

TEACHER to TIM and MIKE   Look, I don't think you'd live if you went in there. I think you'd drown.

TIM to TEACHER   No, we can swim out of them.

TEACHER to TIM   No. Whirlpools are very dangerous.

TIM to TEACHER   On Boris [*a television show*] these baddies got blasted out of a whirlpool in his rocket.

TEACHER to TIM   But that's not possible for you because you're not in a rocket.

TIM to TEACHER   But our boat can turn into a rocket.

TEACHER to TIM   But all you've got are your air tanks.

TIM to TEACHER   And our boat!

As I thought about this conversation, some of the benefits of pretend play became very obvious to me. Tim and Mike were representing their ideas in a variety of forms – through constructing air tanks, drawing a map, as well as expressing their ideas verbally. They were accessing their 'scripts' of scuba diving, and prior knowledge of oceans, weather maps and television shows, and were being challenged by the teacher to assimilate information into their scripts and adapt them to make sense of new information (Katz and Chard, 1989). They were being challenged to imagine consequences and come up with solutions to possible problems even before their pretend game had begun.

As time has progressed, I have become more convinced about the benefits of this type of play. I have also had to think more about the teacher's role in play. The notion of 'scaffolding', as proposed by Bruner (1986) and Vygotsky (Berk and Winsler, 1995), which highlights the idea that a child's existing knowledge base forms a framework from which new knowledge may be learned has been helpful, and I have come to view part of the teacher's role as helping children to tap into their existing knowledge and supporting them in building on this knowledge. I have come to see that this can be done in the context of children's play as the teacher was doing with Tim and Mike. Although my thinking concerning the role of an early childhood teacher has only just begun, my present hope is that I will help children build personal meaning and understanding as they engage in play and express their own ideas. It is from this base that I believe they will come to understand the wider world, and it is for these reasons that I have come to see the value of play.

From these comments it would seem that Rhyll actively sought to challenge and extend her own thinking and understanding. In moving towards a deeper understanding of play, Rhyll had been influenced by some particular theoretical notions derived from her readings, as well as by her observations of practice. As a consequence of extending her understanding of play, Rhyll was also thinking further about her role as a teacher and beginning to articulate her practical theory more clearly.

Considering ethical issues associated with teaching

In considering ethical issues associated with teaching you will ask yourself questions relating to the right and proper ways to conduct yourself when teaching (Katz, 1995b). Although the early childhood profession in a number of countries has developed codes of ethics which are helpful in providing guidelines in this regard, occasions arise in daily teaching experiences which require a teacher to make a personal decision concerning how a particular situation will be handled. Often the decision revolves around the teacher's use of power in relation to a child. David witnessed such an incident during a practicum which he found particularly disturbing and which led him to think deeply about the ethical issues involved. He wrote:

> One morning before class my supervising teacher realized that there was money missing from his desk. (The class had recently been fund raising for an excursion.) He suspected two children who had stolen money previously and called them up to the classroom. One of the children, Darren, was taken inside while the other was told to wait outside. The teacher talked to Darren, and asked him if he knew anything about the missing money. Darren said that he didn't. The teacher, however, said that he knew Darren had taken the money because Byron, the child waiting outside, had told him he had. Darren began to cry and insisted that he had not taken the money. The teacher then talked to Byron, telling him that Darren had told him that he, Byron, had stolen the money. This upset Byron, who became very angry and insisted that he had not taken the money. The teacher then talked to both children telling them they were thieves and that they

should own up to their mistake. Later that afternoon the teacher found the missing money under a pile of books on his desk. He did not say anything to the children.

This incident upset me terribly and made me reconsider the teacher's role. To me the role of the teacher is to be there to provide children with new knowledge and understanding and to provide support for children in this process. In my view the teacher did not provide support for children in this incident. He jumped to conclusions and assumed the two boys were involved in stealing again. I believe that children should not be continually punished for past misbehaviours and should always be given the benefit of the doubt. The way in which the incident was handled caused anger between the teacher and the boys and between the boys themselves. The boys refused to be near each other for the rest of the day and this tension between them continued for the remainder of my prac.

I have learned what not to do from this experience. I have realized that teachers are human and make mistakes, but that it is important that when we do make mistakes we apologize for them. In this case an apology was definitely needed. The children needed to know, and had a right to know, that the money had been found and that they were no longer accused of stealing. I believe this would have lessened the anger.

I have thought about how I would handle such a situation. I think I would talk to the whole class and discuss the problem with all the children. I would talk about how other people are affected when money is stolen. I definitely would not accuse anyone of stealing unless I had witnessed something myself, and I certainly would not lie to children. It was obvious that the two boys were very hurt by the thought that their friend would say such things about them. Having seen the appalling effects of a teacher's unethical and unprofessional conduct I will always try to act ethically.

While it is unlikely that you will witness the type of unethical behaviour that David did because teachers' high standards of professionalism make these types of instances rare, it is useful to reflect on David's experience. This is because, in building your practical theory, you need not only to understand reasons for actions based on theory and observations of practice, but you also need to be able to justify your actions on moral and ethical grounds. In examining his supervising teacher's behaviour in this instance, David high-lighted behaviours which appeared to break an accepted moral code. These behaviours included making accusations without evidence, falsifying the situation, failing to admit his own error and to apologize for perpetrating a hurtful act without justification. While such an incident clearly demonstrates a gross misuse of adult power, you need to be aware that many other 'smaller' incidents can occur which may be counter to an accepted moral code. Issues relating to justice and fairness, labelling children and suspected abuse for example, can challenge you to deal with some difficult ethical dilemmas.

From reading of the experiences of other student teachers and reflecting on their reflections it is hoped that you will have gained some ideas for the way in which you can set about developing your own practical theory of teaching. The key elements in the process are presented in Figure 5.1. Although the elements necessary for developing a practical theory are separated for the purposes of the diagram, like most aspects of teaching they are closely interconnected. For instance, as you describe situations and ask questions you can also be thinking about why things happened the way they did. In discovering reasons for particular responses and consequences you may also be formulating views concerning future strategies you would use in similar situations. At the same time you may well be furthering your knowledge of a particular aspect of learning or teaching either through your readings or observations of practice which may challenge you to revise your teaching strategies. Underlying all your observations and thinking about teaching there must also be a concern for ethical behaviour and an adherence to an accepted moral code.

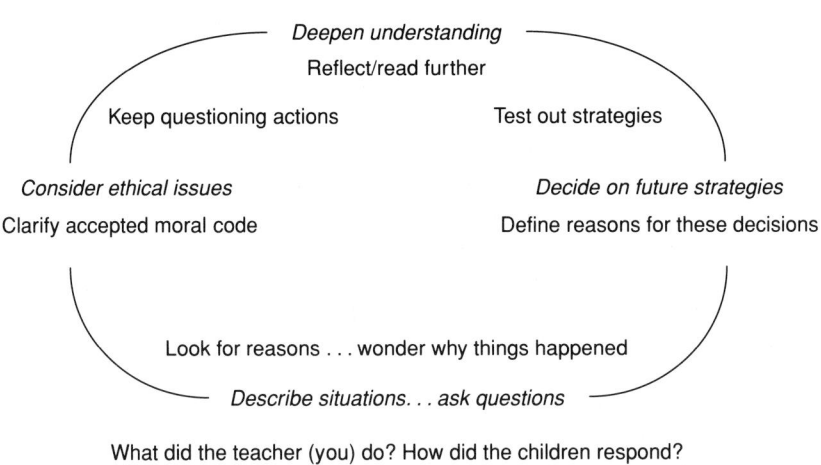

What did the teacher (you) do? How did the children respond?

Figure 5.1 Processes in developing a practical theory

While these elements are in no way seen to be hierarchical, your ability to handle each element will undergo change as your experience and knowledge of teaching increases. As Rose said: 'When I look at the observations I made in first year I'm embarrassed at how little I seemed to see ... and yet at the time I felt I'd made detailed observations.' Such growth and change is at the heart of building your practical theory of teaching. It is important to remember, though, that while you may develop quite a sophisticated practical theory with knowledge of the 'what' and 'how to' of teaching, unless you *use* that knowledge to develop your practical teaching skills it will be of little value to you in classroom situations.

DEVELOPING PRACTICAL SKILLS

What comes to mind when you hear the term 'practical teaching skills'? Some students I asked saw practical teaching skills in terms of 'how to': how to take a group for story or music; teach a language or maths lesson; help the toddler group make the transition from play time to lunch time; talk with children in ways that challenge their thinking. Other students, while agreeing that these were important practical skills, wanted to add different types of skills. These included knowing when and how to intervene, and deciding what to do in a particular situation. Felicity gave as an example an incident where two boys were struggling over who would have the use of the one reel of masking tape on the making table. She said, 'I sat there and watched them and I thought, 'Should I say something, and if I do, what will I say?' She said she spent so much time thinking about the situation that by the time she'd decided she would say something the moment had passed. For Felicity, knowing when and how to intervene was an important practical teaching skill that she wanted to develop. Similarly, Katie said she wanted skills for coping with situations where three or four children were wanting her attention at the one time.

Plate 5.1 Knowing when and how to intervene is an important practical skill. (Photo courtesy of Northgate State Preschool.)

There are many ways in which practical skills can be developed. For instance, you can read about and then practise applying particular teaching techniques such as open-ended questioning, modelling, positive reinforcement, and directive and non-directive statements. You can undertake a micro teaching course and have your teaching videoed so that you can evaluate your skills and have others comment on and discuss your teaching, and you can observe an experienced teacher in action and try to emulate that teacher's actions. Each of these methods can help you become more skilful in particular teaching techniques.

Having a high degree of practical skill in teaching, however, demands more than just having a number of specific practical techniques at your fingertips. It requires you to 'read' situations, to make decisions and to act or respond in the most effective ways in order to promote learning. If these teaching decisions and actions are to be consistent, meaningful for individual children and relevant to particular situations, then you cannot rely on an isolated skill or teaching technique. You must draw on your practical theory. Developing this high level of practical teaching skill by drawing on your practical theory is not easily or quickly achieved. It is a gradual process that comes through critically reflecting on your experiences. A few experiences shared by student teachers may help you get a feel for this process. Their stories illustrate ways in which practical theory has been used to enhance practical teaching skill and to refine teaching actions.

Coping with numerous demands simultaneously

When I visited Katie during her teaching practice she told me that she was feeling very pressured at times. She said:

> I feel I need to be with every child who wants my attention. This morning Ben wanted to make his sandwich for the picnic, and Caitlin wanted me to be in their hospital and Alex came up with his stickle bricks and wanted me to see his building he had made . . . and I knew it was important for each of them that I focus on their needs. . . . I've found that I have to make very quick shifts in my thinking so that I can respond to each of them.

When I asked Katie how she decided to take the action that she did, she said:

> Well . . . it helps that I know the children, and being aware of how they respond helps me decide what I'll do . . . like Ben needs my immediate attention as he just can't wait, while Caitlin and Alex can cope with a little wait. So I knew I had to stay with the sandwich making with Ben . . . and I told Caitlin that I had to make the sandwiches

for the picnic then, but that I would ring her later at the hospital to make an appointment. And I was able to talk to Alex about his building while I helped Ben with his sandwich.

I was wondering whether I was right to give Ben priority just because he was the most likely to make a fuss. When I talked with my teacher about this she said that children like Ben need to know that sometimes other children need your attention first. I think it would take Ben a while to develop that understanding but one of these days I might try saying, 'Ben, I do want to be with you while you make your sandwich but Caitlin needs me in the hospital at the moment, so I'll be here for a little while and then I'll get the butter so you can make the sandwich.' . . . I think I'd have to pick the right moment, though, for Ben to accept that.

In deciding on her course of action Katie was influenced by the 'what' of teaching in her practical theory, recognizing the importance of valuing and attending to each child. On the other hand, she had to deal with the practicalities of the situation. She did this by using her knowledge of each child's behaviour in making her decision about how she would act. Even though her teaching action appeared to be effective, Katie was questioning whether it was right for Ben always to receive her immediate attention. Again she was using her practical theory as a framework against which to consider and refine her teaching actions.

Clarifying teaching actions by reflection

Felicity discovered that she could draw on her practical theory in deciding how to act, although previously she had avoided taking any action at all. As indicated in her example of the tussle between two boys over the use of the one reel of masking tape, Felicity had great difficulty in deciding whether or not to intervene in such situations. As we talked about incidents like this, Felicity indicated that she often felt she should intervene but didn't because she did not know what to say. In discussing this further Felicity agreed that, in relation to such situations, she needed to work out what she could say and why. Together we devised some questions that could guide her reflections, enable her to draw on her practical theory and help her decide on a particular teaching action. These questions were:

- What is my goal for this situation?
- What can I say or do that will help achieve this goal?
- How can I evaluate whether or not my teaching action was successful?

After some reflection Felicity decided that, in relation to the masking-tape incident, her goals could have been to get the boys to talk about their problem and try to come up with a fair solution. She decided that she could have intervened during the tussle by saying, 'There seems to be a problem here . . .'

116

and then asking the children individually what they saw the problem to be. Felicity saw this as a way of getting them to verbalize and accept the problem before asking them for ideas that might 'fix' the problem in a fair way. She thought she could evaluate this teaching action in a number of ways: by the boys' willingness to discuss the problem and to come up with some ideas; the extent to which the ideas were fair; and the actual way in which the situation was resolved.

Even though these reflections occurred after the situation had passed, Felicity said that, having thought through a teaching action, she felt more confident to try it in a similar situation in the future. She also indicated that she was surprised to find that she could draw on her own knowledge, that she had this knowledge tucked away (her practical theory). Now that she knew this knowledge was there Felicity intimated that she might be more confident to step in and say or do something spontaneously if the need arose and reflect on those actions afterwards. Felicity said: 'I haven't done that before because I thought I might have too many negative experiences to reflect on at the end of the day!' Learning to draw on your practical theory not only helps you to develop your practical teaching skills, it can also give you confidence.

Setting teaching goals

Just as Felicity discovered that goal setting could help her formulate her teaching action in relation to a specific situation, Tina discovered that setting herself some broad teaching goals helped her to clarify her thinking about her role when undertaking her teaching practice. Goals are broad statements of what you want to achieve or what the desired end result is (Sebastian-Nickell and Milne, 1992). They can also make recommendations for practice. Løvlie, cited by Handal and Lauvås (1987: 27), suggests that, although goals may not always be written simply, in their most basic form they state, 'As I want to achieve this, then I shall do it this way.' Tina's goals took this form.

After her visiting days at the preschool centre which catered for 3–5-year-old children, Tina said that she felt very confused and 'up in the air about everything'. She felt that if she could set herself some goals that seemed to be consistent with the kind of programme she had seen at the centre, and with her own views about learning and teaching – her practical theory – then she would be clearer about what she should be doing. Her teaching goals, which she wrote in her planning book, indicated that, in order to provide a programme similar to that of her supervising teacher during her teaching practice, she would need to:

- provide varied sensory experiences;
- help children use concepts in solving problems by encouraging intellectual risk taking;

- encourage children to negotiate roles and develop their social relationships;
- promote self-motivation, self-direction and self-regulation.

From talking with Tina about the goals she had set for herself, it was apparent that in trying to achieve these goals she was making some discoveries about the effects of her actions that in turn were helping her to develop and refine her practical teaching skills.

In talking about her goal *to provide varied sensory experiences*, Tina said:

> I was all ready to set up some sensory activities when I realized the very nature of this preschool environment offered the children so many . . . going barefoot in the sand . . . digging in the mud patch . . . picking up the leaves . . . playing the musical instruments. It was what they were learning while they were doing these things . . . I realized that was more important than just providing the experiences . . . and I found I could help them be more aware of what they were sensing by talking about it. I tried saying, 'I wonder why autumn leaves are yellow? and . . . the sound of that instrument makes me think of. . . .' It was good to develop that practical skill of talking with children in a way that helped them wonder about things.

In reflecting on her goal *to help children solve problems*, Tina felt she had encouraged the children in this regard although her role mainly had been a

Plate 5.2 While providing sensory experiences is important, talking with children about what they are sensing is also important. (Photo courtesy of Chapel Hill Kindergarten.)

supportive one because children were used to being problem solvers. She talked about how she had supported Andrew who wanted to take the large hollow blocks up to the fort in the top part of the playground. She said,

> He was faced with the problem of how to get the blocks there ... and so we talked about several ways he could do it. He decided to use the trolley ... I don't think he really knew the problems he was up against. I knew I'd have to be there to support him ... to get him to think of some ways he could overcome the problems.

Tina felt she had spent more time with the 3–4-year-old group than the older group in *encouraging them to build social relationships*. She said,

> I seem to spend a lot of time helping them to be aware of others' feelings. Like with Jeff, when he was punching, or constantly wanting his own way ... I would just try to spend as much time with him as I could when a situation arose. ... Like at the dough table when he grabbed another child's play dough, I'd just talk about sharing, and ... just try to do it informally. I realized you can't set an activity for something like that. You just have to be there at the right moment and talk over what's expected. I guess I've become more skilful at making the most of those moments!

In terms of *promoting self-motivation, self-direction and self regulation*, I was surprised when Tina said she felt she 'hadn't done much', because her planning was full of examples where she had helped the children follow through on their interests and encouraged their self-direction and motivation. We talked about Sandi and the shop she had made during my visit. Tina said that the day before, Sandi was in the sandpit and was desperately trying to get the shop going.

> Sandi is very outspoken and she was saying, 'I want to sell chocolate cakes' ... but none of the other children was interested ... and I could see she was getting flustered because the others usually do what she wants. It was nearly the end of the session so I didn't follow it up then but I thought I would for tomorrow. So last night I thought about the things she might like to use in her shop. When she came this morning I said, 'There are some things near the sandpit that you might be able to use to get a shop going today.'
>
> I guess I was thinking about how we could go about developing the shop ... what Sandi could do with it ... who might join her ... what she might learn from it ... and I guess that what I was hoping she would learn would be cooperation with others ... and knowing that her idea is worth something. I can see now that, because it did turn out to be a positive experience for her, it will give her more motivation and self-direction in future. ... I just hadn't thought of it like that before.

There's just so much to think about. Honestly, when I first started this course I did think I'd be able to learn everything in a few years ... but I can see now that's not possible.

For Tina, the setting of teaching goals helped her gain new insights about teaching, and assisted her to develop her practical skills as she planned, engaged in and reflected on experiences that were designed to achieve her goals. Her practical theory helped her define her goals, and, in working towards them, she was examining the nature of her teaching and refining her practical teaching skills. When I asked Tina why she opted for a particular teaching action rather than another (for example, why she decided that it was better to talk with Jeff about hitting during 'his moments' rather than having a group discussion about hitting at a later time), she said she wasn't sure. In some instances she knew she was using strategies that had 'worked' for her before or that she had seen other teachers use effectively. On other occasions she tried out particular techniques she had read about or heard other students talk about. As she thought about this question some more, she said that she guessed her decisions had something to do with what she understood about how children learned, but that she had never really thought about why she opted for some teaching actions rather than others. This led us to think about how teachers decide whether one way of teaching or handling a situation is better than another.

USING PRACTICAL THEORY TO REFINE PRACTICAL SKILLS

I had an opportunity to consider this question of how decisions are made concerning whether one way of teaching is better than another when I undertook some research in a double unit preschool, catering for 4–5-year-olds some years ago (Perry, 1988). Both teachers in that preschool believed strongly that the learning experiences they provided should foster the children's active participation and be related to their interests and needs. I happened to be observing in the centre in the week in which the local fire brigade had agreed to visit as a follow-up to the children's interests in firemen. I was fascinated to observe the different ways in which these two preschool teachers went about preparing the children for the visit, as well as the way in which the visit was followed up. Here are some of my observations:

Cathy, the teacher in Unit One, told the children at the morning discussion group that the fire brigade was going to visit their preschool on Tuesday. The children seemed interested and John asked if they would bring their fire engine. The teacher said they would, and then proceeded to show the children some pictures of firemen in action which she had previously selected. She asked the children what they could see happening in the pictures, and some of the children replied with the obvious answers, 'They're putting out the fire,' 'He's holding the hose,' 'They're wearing their helmets.' The teacher looked pleased when they gave their 'right' answers and often repeated what a child had said ... 'Yes, they're putting out the fire.' There was no further questioning once an answer had been given. After they had looked at the six pictures Cathy said she would put the pictures up on the wall so they could have a closer look at them later in the day. She then said she was going to read them a story about firemen. The story was somewhat dated, with stylized illustrations of old-time fire engines. The children seemed interested, however, and listened attentively. There was no further discussion at the end of the story and I didn't hear any more comments from the children about the firemen's visit during their play, although I noticed two children individually pause to take a closer look at the pictures the teacher had pinned on the wall.

What are your initial reactions to such observations? In reflecting on the teacher's actions I thought here was a teacher who was well organized – having the pictures and story ready, and who was keen to prepare the children for the visit by giving them information about what firemen do and the equipment they use. I did wonder what the children got from the discussion. Did they discover anything they didn't already know? I wondered, too, about whether the outdated story and illustrations could have caused any confusion in relation to the children's own knowledge of fire engines. The children had, however, appeared very focused as they listened to the story. When I talked briefly with the teacher about this session she said she had wanted to give the children some specific information about firemen and that by 'discussing' the pictures, all the children had an opportunity to be actively involved. Overall, I thought this discussion and story time was like many I had taken and had seen other teachers take. I had cause for much more thought, however, when I saw how the teacher in Unit Two introduced the visit.

Joan, the teacher in Unit Two, also told the children about the forthcoming visit of the fire brigade at the group discussion. The children were impressed. Timothy said, 'Wow! That's exciting,' and David asked, 'Will they show us the siren?' The group discussed David's question and decided that they would. The teacher said, 'I wonder what the firemen will bring with them?' With that leading question, the discussion took off. The children suggested all kinds of possibilities ... 'hoses', 'their helmets', 'their axes' (what did they need those for?) 'their radios'. . . . They also wondered about what they would wear and why firemen needed to wear different clothes when they were fighting fires. Nearly all the children in the group contributed either a suggestion or comment to the discussion and each child's idea was listened to and treated with respect. Sometimes the teacher had to ensure that an idea was heard by saying, 'That's an interesting thought, Naomi. Did you all hear what Naomi suggested?' There were a number of 'I wonders' left hanging, with the teacher suggesting, 'We'll have to especially look for that,' or 'That's an interesting question. You'll need to ask the fireman about that.' At lunch I heard a few children continuing to discuss the visit, with David saying, ' I hope they let us sit up the front in the engine part' and Martin replying that he didn't think they would.

What do you see as some of the main differences between Cathy's and Joan's approach in this introductory session? From my observations Joan seemed keen to build on the children's knowledge, but she needed to discover what knowledge they had first. A few key 'wonderings' concerning what the firemen would bring and wear were sufficient to spark the children's thinking so that they began to access and contribute their own knowledge of firemen. They seemed more actively involved than the children in the other Unit. I found it interesting that, at this stage, Joan did not seek to *give* information through pictures or reading a story. Instead she sought to establish what the children knew and what they wanted to find out. When I spoke briefly with Joan concerning her goals for this introductory session, she said that she wanted the children to do their own thinking about firemen, to share what knowledge they had, and to hear what ideas the other children might have about the firemen and their visit. She also said that this type of discussion gave her glimpses of individual children's ways of thinking and understanding.

Would you agree that, at this point, there seemed to be some fundamental differences between these two teaching approaches? Cathy wanted to give the children information and Joan wanted the children to realize what they already knew, what they wanted to know, and how they could find out. I was not at the preschool the day the firemen visited, but I did observe the follow-up discussions on the day after the visit. The different ways in which these discussions were handled provided more challenges to my thinking.

Cathy began the discussion with her group by saying, 'Well, did you enjoy the firemen's visit yesterday?' All the children chorused 'Yes'. Cathy then said, 'David, what did you like best about the visit?' David replied that he'd liked the siren. Cathy said, 'Yes, I liked that too. Mark, what did you like?' All the children in the group were asked individually what they had liked and most came up with three- or four-word answers. . . . 'I liked their helmets,' 'the hoses', 'their radio thing'. There was a deal of repetition as some children reiterated what others had said and there was no discussion or elaboration on the children's likes. It was a question-and-answer situation which ended with the teacher saying, 'Well, you might like to pretend you're firemen during inside time today.' Cathy then explained the other activities that were available.

In contrast, the discussion in Joan's Unit was a real sharing of what both the teacher and the children had learned and had found interesting.

> Joan began the discussion by saying, 'Well, I learned lots of new things about firemen yesterday. I didn't know that they sometimes wore masks, did you?' Nicholas said, 'Yeah, I did. But the mask felt funny when I put it on.' Joan responded, 'Did it? What did it feel like, Nicholas?' Nicholas searched for words, 'Well ... it felt ... all over my face.' There were many spontaneous comments. 'I liked ... sitting high up in the front part ... holding the hose ... seeing the axe ... the badge on the coat ...', with children being encouraged to express why they had liked particular aspects. During the discussion the teacher introduced some books and pictures which were used as a basis for comparison. Joan would say, 'In the picture the fire engine has the hose stored on the side here. Is that where the hose was on our fire engine?' 'This seems to be a different type of siren. What's different about this siren, from the one we saw?' The children quickly became engrossed in pointing out similarities and differences, debating the finer points, not only with the teacher but also with each other. At the conclusion of the discussion when the children were talking about their games for inside time, several indicated that they were going to be firemen. Joan discussed with them where they were going to build their fire engines and what materials they might need.

As I reflected on these two follow-up discussions I realized that they had provided very different experiences for the children in each Unit. Cathy's children certainly got to state their likes and hear other children's likes, but what other opportunities for learning were there? The question-and-answer format of the session afforded no opportunities for the children to express the reasons for their preferences or to share their wonderings. From being able to observe these two different approaches I came to realize how important it is for teachers to question critically whether their actions are achieving their goals. I recalled that when I was teaching, like Cathy, I had sincerely believed children should be actively involved in their own learning. Because I had led discussions in a way similar to Cathy's, however, I had probably kept the children's participation to a superficial level. It was only as I had the opportunity to observe and think about Joan's approach that I came to see a 'better' way of leading a discussion.

In Joan's Unit the children were able to build on their previous knowledge of firemen. Because the introductory session had helped the children to organize their own thinking and to feel confident in their role as learners and questioners they were prepared to ask the firemen questions and discover new knowledge. The excitement of these discoveries was shared by both teacher and children in the follow-up session as they communicated their thoughts and feelings. The introduction of the pictures after the children had clarified their own knowledge seemed to provide a further stimulus for discussion, encouraging children to make more connections as well as to search for similarities and differences.

In trying to clarify why Joan's approach so appealed to me, an immediate reaction was to state my reasons in terms of the children's more active participation, the sharing and organization of their existing knowledge and their delight in the discovery of new knowledge. The observations seemed to provide 'evidence' of effective teaching and learning. As I thought about my reasons some more, however, I realized that my view of the 'evidence' was also being influenced by theoretical understandings of the benefits of promoting multiple learnings – assisting children to learn three or four things at the same time (Fortson and Reiff, 1995). Joan was not only furthering the children's knowledge about firemen but also doing it in ways which enabled children to:

- communicate their own thoughts and feelings;
- make discoveries about what they did or did not know;
- work out ways to ask questions and gather more information;
- feel confident in their role as learners and questioners;
- share the excitement of making new discoveries;
- search for similarities and differences.

All these learnings were contributing to the broader competencies necessary for successful living. From my theoretical knowledge I recognized that today's children – tomorrow's adults – will not only require content knowledge but they also will need to have 'cope-ability', and to be flexible, resourceful, enquiring and responsible (Toffler, 1974). This theoretical knowledge, then, indicated the importance of teaching competencies that provide the foundations for success throughout life while at the same time teaching specific information. In thinking about why Joan's teaching approach so appealed to me, then, I was drawing on the observed 'practice', the children's responses and theoretical reasons. I was using my practical theory to reconsider and refine teaching strategies for leading discussion groups. It was a process that challenged me to change and grow as a teacher.

SUMMARY

In developing your understanding of what teaching is and how it can be undertaken you are developing your practical theory of teaching. This chapter has highlighted a number of ways in which you can further your understanding of the 'what' and 'how to' of teaching. These include:

- asking questions about your own teaching actions;
- clarifying reasons for the particular responses of children to your actions;

- being prepared to challenge and extend your existing knowledge about teaching at a practical and theoretical level;
- considering ethical issues associated with teaching.

In order to develop a high level of practical skill, you need to be able to *use* your knowledge of the 'what' and 'how to' of teaching. Although becoming skilled in particular teaching techniques such as questioning, modelling and positive reinforcement is important, teaching also requires that you be able to 'read' situations and make decisions that enable you to use the most appropriate strategies for individual children in particular situations. In order to make these types of decisions you must draw on your knowledge of the 'what' and 'how to' of teaching – on your practical theory. Your practical theory, then, provides you with a framework within which you opt for a particular course of action, decide when to use a particular teaching technique – or combination of techniques – and consider how your teaching strategies can be refined. If you are prepared to use your practical theory in this way you can expect not only challenges but also growth in your understanding and skill as a teacher.

SUGGESTED ACTIVITIES

- In small groups of two or three, take turns to describe a situation that, in your view, exemplifies 'good teaching'. Discuss each example and see if your views coincide, or whether there are some differences in your views about what is good teaching. Note the similarities and differences in your thinking. List some reasons for particular views.

- Select a topic related to teaching which is of particular interest to you (for instance, helping children problem solve; resolve conflict; bullying; the teacher's role in play; developing number concepts; emergent literacy). Prior to teaching practice undertake readings on the topic, and during teaching practice take every opportunity to observe, and extend your knowledge and experience in relation to it. After teaching practice, summarize what you have learned concerning the topic and indicate how your teaching practices have changed as a result of your new knowledge.

- In small groups share and discuss an ethical dilemma that you have experienced, or alternatively, an ethical dilemma you perceive or have heard talked about. Consider the factors that are contributing to the dilemma, and write down possible ways of handling the situation including the people from whom you could seek advice.

- Think about and describe a particular teaching strategy you use (for example, the way you settle a group, read a story, help a child to feel worthwhile and valued). Observe another teacher's handling of a similar situation or talk with your peers about their particular strategies. Critically reflect on what you do in the light of these observations or discussions as well as your theoretical knowledge. Decide whether or not you want to make changes to your teaching strategy and give reasons for your decision.

- What are some of the most important aspects of your approach to teaching? Spend some time writing them down and then outline them to one of your peers and in the process explain why they are important to you. (If you can do this, you are well on the way in developing your practical theory. Remember, though, this practical theory will change as you gain experience.)

6

WORKING WITH ADULTS IN EARLY CHILDHOOD SETTINGS

In this chapter consideration will be given to:

- ways of building an effective working relationship with your supervising teacher;
- getting to know the organizational structure of the setting and working as a member of a team;
- how cooperation between teachers and parents can be developed.

As a teacher you will be required to develop and maintain effective and collaborative working relationships with colleagues, families, volunteers and other professionals associated with your school or centre. Teaching practice gives you the opportunity to observe these relationships in action. As well, your teaching practice experiences enable you to become familiar with the organizational structure of a variety of settings. This structure has a bearing on working relationships. For instance, particular people will occupy particular positions to which expectations are attached. The principal or director, for example, is expected to provide overall leadership, cleaners are required to do their set tasks at certain times, while aides or assistants support classroom teachers. Beside this more *formal* organizational structure there is also the *informal* structure of the setting (Cohen and Manion, 1993). This is a network of social relationships developed by staff, regardless of their positions, as they chat in the staff room, exchange 'news' in the corridors, or participate in school activities. Becoming aware of both the formal and informal organizational structures of your practice teaching setting will help you to understand better the nature of the relationships and the factors that contribute to their effectiveness.

As well as enabling you to observe and experience the effects of organizational structures, teaching practice gives you the opportunity to gain skill in developing your own effective working relationships. For instance, it is important that you establish a positive relationship with your supervising teacher. Depending on the type of setting you are in, there may also be opportunities for you to establish collaborative relationships with an aide or other members of staff. Although your supervising teacher will be as keen as you are to develop an effective working relationship, other staff members may not have the time to be as collaborative as they may wish. If the teaching practice is short, be realistic about the type of relationships that can be established in a limited time. Sometimes, in some teaching practice situations, you have to be content to observe 'relationships' from the sidelines. You can learn a lot from such observations, just as you can learn about building relationships in general, from developing your relationship with your supervising teacher.

DEVELOPING AN EFFECTIVE RELATIONSHIP WITH YOUR SUPERVISING TEACHER

Wondering how you will 'get on' with your supervising teacher is likely to be uppermost in your mind as you make your initial contact with staff in the centre where you will undertake your teaching practice. Often that first meeting is the hardest hurdle to overcome. Samantha-Lee described her experience this way:

> The memory of my first visit to the school where I was to do my final year teaching practice will linger throughout my teaching career. Those moments of introducing myself to the Deputy Principal, administration staff and supervising teacher seemed to last forever. My mind charged ahead of me as I tried to envisage what might happen next, what people might say and how I could respond in a professional way. I so wanted to be seen as a keen, industrious and pleasant student.
>
> I had thought about what I wanted to learn during this prac. I needed to sift through my developing knowledge base and apply strategies in practice that looked so good in my assignments. I wanted to reflect on my own philosophies of teaching, be able to take risks, experiment with ideas and explore personal ideologies about children and their learning. I also wanted to interact more with other staff members, to learn about their experiences, feelings and attitudes and gain some helpful advice. I felt ready to involve myself in extra-curricular activities so I said 'Yes' when these opportunities were offered, and agreed to umpire school netball, attend school meetings and assist in the organization of the cross country.

The importance of communication in building relationships

Samantha-Lee had prepared for her initial visit by thinking about the image of herself as a student that she wanted to communicate. She had also clarified what she hoped to gain from her teaching practice and was able to share these goals with her teacher. Fortunately for Samantha-Lee, her supervising teacher was happy to support her in working towards her goals. Samantha-Lee said:

My teacher made it clear from the start, that, as I was in my final year, she would provide me with space and flexibility. She encouraged me to work on my ideas and respond to children as I thought best. She let me deal with the difficult situations and helped me to engage in more self-reflection. I responded positively to this approach although underneath I was quite fearful, particularly at the thought of being 'in control' and planning a full unit of work. My teacher reassured me that I was more than ready to do this. This built my confidence and in the process I became aware of my own needs and abilities.

The relationship Samantha-Lee and her supervising teacher built was a very positive one. There appear to be a number of factors that contributed to its development:

- they each were aware of the importance of clear communication;
- they prepared for the teaching practice by clarifying their own expectations and possible actions;
- they shared common goals;
- they each expressed ideas as to how these goals might be achieved;
- they respected each other's contribution to the relationship (e.g., the teacher respected Samantha-Lee's keen attitude and her willingness to take on challenges, while Samantha-Lee appreciated the teacher's confidence and trust in her abilities and the opportunities to make her own dis-coveries).

Being a final year student, Samantha-Lee was able to draw on her previous experiences of building relationships in preparing herself for her final teaching practice. As you gain experience, you, too, will find it useful to think about the factors that have contributed to effective working relationships with supervising teachers. Be prepared to learn from your less positive experiences as well.

Because students and supervising teachers have different personalities and communicative abilities and experience so many differing needs and pressures, the student–supervising teacher relationship does not always develop effectively. Sometimes your supervising teacher may perceive a particular problem or weakness, or you may feel that your teacher's expectations or demands are unreasonable. Although when looked at objectively it seems that it should be relatively easy to talk with each other about these problems, in practice it is quite difficult. It is useful to think about why this is, because by understanding the reasons for the difficulty, you will be in a better position to overcome it.

Sometimes, even though you may sense there is a problem, it is hard to identify what the problem is. Even when you are able to clarify the nature of the problem, it is not always easy to admit your part in it to yourself, let alone to another person. This is because we tend to look at problems in terms of 'failures' rather than seeing them as a means of learning. Even some super-vising teachers find it difficult to talk with students about students' problems because they see themselves 'failing' to help the student. Frequently, discus-sion of the difficulties gets left until a third person, such as the principal or director, intervenes or the university teacher visits. Probably because this third person is outside the working relationship, both teacher and student find it easier to discuss their concerns with this outside person. I experienced this type of discussion recently with a few supervising teachers, who, in talking about the progress of their students, also expressed some concerns. For example:

- Miss T said that Dale seemed to ignore her suggestions for planning a lesson.
- Anne was concerned that her student, John, didn't provide or make resources that would enrich children's experiences.
- Mrs S indicated that Angela managed time poorly – the children's time and her own.

When I spoke with each student about the particular issue their supervising teacher had raised, they all agreed that a problem did exist and could understand their supervising teacher's concerns. I was fascinated to discover that in talking about the problem with me, each student could see possible ways of working through the problem or of resolving it. Not one of them, however, had discussed these possible solutions with their supervising teacher. For instance, Dale said:

> I know Miss T thinks I'm not taking notice of what she says when she tells me how to plan a lesson, but honestly ... I don't know what she's talking about half the time. There's so many things she says I should do ... my mind just shuts off. She keeps mentioning these words ... like 'orientating' and 'enhancing phases of the lesson' ... and because she thinks I know their meaning, I'm not game to ask her what she means. If she'd just focus on one or two things I should do each lesson ... I think I could cope with that ... or if she gave me a sample lesson plan ... that might help.

As we talked further, it was evident that Dale's supervising teacher expected her to plan her lessons in a particular way and to incorporate more into her lessons than Dale felt able to do. Her supervising teacher didn't ask Dale how she felt about what was being asked of her, and Dale felt unable to say she didn't understand or could only deal with a certain amount at one time. Because of this lack of communication, frustrations built for both Dale and her teacher. There was an obvious need for Dale to be more honest in communicating to her teacher about what she did and did not understand. We talked about how Dale could do this through her use of 'I' messages (Gordon, 1974), which would indicate to her teacher that she recognized it as *her* problem. We also discussed some possible 'I' messages she could use (for example, 'I don't understand some of the terms you use to describe the lesson phases. Could you explain them to me please?' 'I'm having difficulty including all the things you ask me to do in my lesson plan. For tomorrow, could I focus on just two of the aspects you've suggested?'). Dale agreed to try this approach and later told me that, although she felt she still had not met the teacher's expectations, her more honest approach in communicating her difficulties had helped them to develop a more effective working relationship.

In talking with John, he agreed that his teacher's concern at his lack of resources for his lessons was justified. He said:

> Anne's right in saying I don't provide resources ... it's because I work each afternoon in after school care and go home to the farm to help my parents at weekends. I don't have a chance to get to the Uni library ... or the resource centre, and by the time I do my planning and written work at night I don't have time to make any ... besides I couldn't afford to buy the materials.

Lack of communication between John and his teacher seemed to lie at the heart of this problem too. When I asked John if he had explained his situation to Anne, he said he hadn't because it sounded like he was making excuses. As we talked about it some more, however, John realized that by explaining his situation he wasn't making excuses, but was, in fact, honestly sharing with Anne some of his 'realities'. On his return to campus he told me that he did talk to Anne about his situation and that she seemed to appreciate his sharing of his difficulty. Anne had helped him to access the school library. The librarian had not only provided him with some useful resources but had also increased his awareness of how children and teachers could make the most of the library within the school. In reviewing his teaching practice, John wrote:

> I've learned that sharing difficulties is not necessarily seen as making excuses. This experience has shown me that it is necessary to share something of yourself, including your problems, if you are going to build a trusting and supportive relationship.

Angela, in talking about her difficulty in managing time, said that this had always been a problem for her. She said:

> All my life I've had trouble with time. I sit down to write my plans as soon as I get home ... and they just take me hours. I must spend a lot of time just thinking because I don't have that much on paper to show for it. Then, even though I plan a lesson carefully, when I actually give it, I find that something I thought would take ten minutes has only taken three, or something I thought the children would do quickly takes

them ages. So I'm either finished way before the bell is due to go, or the children are just getting involved when it's lunch time. I know Mrs S doesn't think I'm a very good organizer, and I can see why. I'm trying to plan extra activities so I've got something prepared if we finish early ... but I'm not sure how I can stop running over time.

We talked about the possibility of Angela's asking Mrs S to look at her plans and help her estimate more accurately the time needed for particular activities. At the conclusion of her teaching practice Angela told me that she did this and that Mrs S had been very helpful. She said:

Once I broke the ice and asked her advice on estimating the time for different activities, I found I could ask her questions about a lot of other things. We had some very helpful discussions ... and she gave me a lot of useful information. She even had some suggestions for managing my own time when planning ... like giving myself ten minutes to come up with three objectives and strategies for a particular lesson.

From these discussions with students about the concerns raised by their supervising teachers, a number of aspects relating to the nature of verbal communication necessary in building effective relationships emerge. They provide some helpful guidelines for communicating in ways which will help you build your relationship with your supervising teacher.

- *Be open and honest in sharing your own thinking or perceptions of situations.* If you don't understand what is being said or asked of you, use 'I' messages to clarify meanings and expectations, or to indicate what you feel you can do.
- *Be prepared to talk about the realities or difficulties of your situation.* Provided that you do not use your difficulties to make excuses, talking about them will help your supervising teacher better understand what you are facing. Often, when difficulties are shared, they are more easily overcome because two heads are better than one in finding solutions!
- *Seek specific information and guidance whenever possible.* The more specific you can be in asking a question or seeking information, the more likely it is that you will receive a relevant and meaningful answer. Remember, too, that once you have broken the ice by asking a question or seeking advice, the easier and more natural this process becomes.

The importance of positive attitudes in building relationships

In some instances negative attitudes or emotions that have not been dealt with can be the cause of difficulties in developing effective student–supervising teacher relationships. This proved to be the case for Diane and Karley. Diane's teacher was concerned that Diane stood back and did not interact easily with preschool children, while Karley's teacher told me that Karley seemed to freeze in some situations, so that children quickly became out of control.

When I talked with Diane about her teacher's concern over her lack of involvment with the children, Diane said that she was feeling overwhelmed, not only by her first experience of teaching practice, but also because of some personal problems. She said:

> I moved out of home last week into a flat with some friends. I've never lived away from home before and I've had to get my furniture organized and . . . I've been so busy thinking about all those things I'm having difficulty focusing on prac . . . and anyway, I'm not really sure that I want to be an early childhood teacher. I can see my teacher is committed to what she does. When I came to this preschool I realized just how much a teacher has to do . . . like be friends with parents . . . know children . . . be aware of home backgrounds. You must get a lot from doing that . . . and that's the kind of job I think I want . . . a job with a challenge . . . but I'm just not sure.

Diane was discovering that it is difficult to give your best effort to teaching practice when you are coping with a lot of personal problems. For Diane her personal difficulties were compounded by her uncertainty about whether or not she wanted to be a teacher. She was dealing with so many personal thoughts and emotions that she was unable to focus on her teaching practice responsibilities and remained uninvolved. As we talked, Diane came to the view that, although sharing all her personal problems with her teacher would be inappropriate, it was only fair that her supervising teacher know something of her difficulties and her uncertainties about being a teacher. She felt this would help her teacher understand her lack of emotional commitment. She also wanted her teacher to know that the difficulties preventing the development of a working relationship were not of the teacher's making. I don't know whether or not Diane shared her difficulties with her supervising teacher, but I learned later that she had deferred her teaching practice and was talking with the student counsellor before making any decisions about her future career. I was pleased that Diane had taken action to help resolve her dilemmas and had gone to the appropriate person – the student counsellor.

When I talked with Karley about her teacher's concerns, she agreed that in some situations she just 'froze'. She said:

> I seem to freeze while I try to work out something to say that won't offend anyone. From Uni and all the subjects . . . I've got all this information in my head that conflicts with my natural feelings, which are what I've been taught as a child. Like I was told 'be quiet', 'go to the corner' . . . which didn't make me think about what I had done wrong . . . it just made me cranky . . . and when a child is being difficult I go to do what comes naturally . . . and then I think about

my lectures ... and I know what I'm thinking of doing is wrong ... and then I feel a bit nervous because I haven't reacted straight away because I have to think about those two things ... and I just stand there. But I think I know my teacher well enough now to talk to her about this.

Karley did talk with her teacher about her difficulty. On her return to the University she told me that she had opened up the conversation by saying: I'm really confused about discipline. ... I don't know whether it does anything to send a child away from the group. ... I can see that you can't have one child totally disrupting the class ... but I was wondering is there something better? By opening the conversation with this 'I' message, Karley was indicating that she wanted to think more about the purpose and nature of effective discipline. She indicated that her teacher had responded by sharing her thoughts about promoting self-discipline. Karley had written many of her teacher's comments in her journal:

My teacher said that in any group situation you've got to have some sense of order and control and that what she was aiming for was for children to have self-control. She said there were many ways of helping children achieve this. Some of her suggestions were:

- to explain to children why some behaviours are acceptable and others are not;
- to encourage the children to help make rules ... but only to have a few, and to make sure they are reasonable and positive ones;
- to use praise effectively by stating the desired behaviour (e.g., 'That was thoughtful to move up to make a space for Joe in the circle');
- to warn children of the logical consequences that will follow if rules are broken but to do this in a way that allows the child to make a choice (e.g., 'Either you sit here quietly and keep your hands in your lap ... or you will have to sit over there by yourself');
- to follow through on warnings if the child doesn't comply.

Karley said she had found this discussion very helpful. She had come to realize that, as a child, she had not been given any reasons as to why her behaviour was unacceptable. Nor had she been given any warnings or choice. Although she still did not feel comfortable about 'disciplining' children because of her own experiences, she was coming to see that achieving self-control was an important aspect of children's learning. Karley said that she recognized that the discipline strategies the teacher used seemed likely to help the children. She still felt her own stress levels rise, however, when she observed these situations, and realized she would have to do a lot more reading, talking and thinking about the topic in order to build her understanding and come to terms with her own past experiences. She recognized that she needed to sort through her feelings in order to use positive guidance strategies with children effectively.

Although this discussion about supervising teachers' concerns may suggest that supervising teachers are hard to please, this is not true. In my experience, in any round of teaching practice visits there are many more 'delighted' supervising teachers than 'concerned' ones. I recently asked three experienced supervising teachers what type of attitudes they valued in students. Their comments may help you look at the student–supervising teacher relationship from the supervising teacher's perspective.

Fay said:

> I enjoy having students who show me that they have a real interest in teaching and a real interest in children. I like students to ask me questions that show me they are thinking about what they are seeing . . . or that help them build on the knowledge they have already gained. Another reason I like them asking questions is because I know that they're interested in what we're talking about . . . and it's not just something that I'm interested in.

Jan said:

> I particularly value those who come with an open mind. I've had students who've come and said, 'On this prac I have to do this and I have to do that.' They haven't stopped to look at what the centre might have to offer them, nor have they thought about some of the additional things they might learn. They seem to have blinkers on and only attempt to meet the set requirements. I find it frustrating working with students who put limits on their own learning.

Gay agreed. She said:

> Yes. That's why I've really enjoyed having Louise this prac. She's treated prac as a valuable experience in itself . . . not as something to 'get through'. She's thought about her prac requirements but she's met the requirements in ways that have ensured that she has added to her understanding. She's been at a stage where she will notice something and can verbalize her thoughts about what she sees and I can talk about how I see that situation. We've had some interesting discussions. It's been a valuable experience for both of us.

These examples and comments, then, provide you with some guidelines concerning the types of attitudes that will help you build an effective relationship with your supervising teacher.

- *Aim to be free of personal problems during teaching practice.* Try to deal with personal issues prior to teaching practice. Should personal difficulties overwhelm you, seek help from a counsellor. It is not reasonable to burden your supervising teacher with your personal problems.
- *Be prepared to think through your own childhood experiences in the light of your new knowledge.* If, for example, you are going to give children

positive guidance and support you will need to feel comfortable with yourself and what you are doing. Talk with your teacher about strategies that can be used and the reasons for their use. You may also need to 'confront' some of your more negative past experiences. Seek help from a student counsellor if necessary.

• *Enter teaching practice with an open mind.* Remember that your learning can go beyond meeting the set requirements. As you build different relationships with different supervising teachers, you will find that each has particular strengths which may influence your own practice. Seek to discover a variety of perspectives on teaching issues and remain open to persuasive arguments.

BECOMING FAMILIAR WITH ORGANIZATIONAL STRUCTURES AND RELATIONSHIPS

Because the organizational structure of each teaching practice setting will differ due to its size, type of administration and style of leadership, it is important that you seek advice from your supervising teacher concerning the particular aspects of your setting, with which you should become familiar. In this way, as you gain experience in different early childhood settings you will be acquainted with various aspects of organization and a range of roles and relationships. As a beginning student teacher you may find it easier to focus on roles and relationships within your own classroom. By your final teaching practice, however, you should be familiar with the roles of all members of staff as well as the administrative and organizational aspects of the school or centre. In this section a small sample of students' and supervising teachers' experiences will be presented so as to illustrate how your understanding of roles and relationships can be increased during teaching practice.

The teacher–aide relationship

Gay, one of the experienced teachers I talked with, indicated that she wanted her student to understand the role of the aide and the nature of the teacher–aide relationship because it was an important aspect of her preschool's organizational setting. She said:

> I think it's important for students to realize that aides really do have to know what's going on ... even if some of the information you pass on seems trivial ... so that things run smoothly. For instance, if I don't pass on a telephone message about Jack's grandfather picking him up instead of his mother, then there could be confusion between the aide and Jack's grandparent at going home time.
>
> I also think that students need to know that your aide is an important member of the teaching team. In this centre my aide, Agnes, is

constantly interacting with the children ... and I need to share my goals for the children with her so we can work together. We chat about these things before and after the session ... and I've included my student in these discussions so she can experience how information can be shared. I also encourage Agnes to share her perceptions of the children and how they have handled particular situations. I really value her observations. When my student plans a particular experience I ask her to explain her plans to Agnes as well as how she would like Agnes to assist her. I know she has found this difficult to do ... because Agnes is so much older and more experienced than she is ... but I think it is important that a student learns how to do this ... in a collaborative kind of way.

Plate 6.1 Aides are important members of the teaching team continually interacting with children. (Photo courtesy of Northgate State Preschool.)

Louise, Gay's student, agreed that she had found it difficult to explain to Agnes, the aide, what she planned to do and how Agnes could assist. She realized, however, that an aide had to understand the teacher's goals if the assistance was to be effective. Louise also said that she had to be 'extra clear' in her own mind about her plans if her explanations were to be helpful to Agnes. She said, 'It was a scary . . . but useful thing to do.'

The role of a day-care centre director

Although Bronwyn, a final year student, was doing her teaching practice with the babies and toddlers in a day-care centre, Cathy, the director, suggested that Bronwyn should also become familiar with the director's role. Cathy assisted Bronwyn in this by sharing with her some of her activities. Bronwyn noted these activities together with some observations in her journal:

29 July

Cathy demonstrated leadership skills as she oriented me to the centre, talking about the reasons underlying the set up of the environment. She lent me the Staff Policy Handbook and gave me a folder of information about the centre.

Cathy works 'from' her office rather than 'in' her office. There is no desk – just chairs side by side to help people feel more relaxed.

12 August

Cathy put up a notice to parents reminding them of the need for punctuality when picking up children. The notice board carried an additional large, red-lettered PLEASE READ sign which was effective.

Jamie was discovered to have a sore eye, possibly conjunctivitis. Cathy contacted his parent. Jamie was 'isolated' in his pram from other children but was comforted by B until his mother arrived.

28 August

Cathy came to the babies' room to settle a child who was very upset because the regular carer was away. Needs of the children take precedence over whatever else is on Cathy's agenda.

29 August

Fire drill held today (occurs approximately once a month). Staff gather children and move to the gate in the over 3's area. Babies are carried in arms. The roll is called.

Cathy talked about staff–parent relations with a staff member who had experienced a confrontation with a parent recently. The staff member later commented in the staff room that she had appreciated Cathy's support and caring attitude.

4 Sept

Staff have one and a half hours for programming each week. Cathy attends when possible. In the session I attended:

• Daily sheets from babies' room (solids, fluids, sleep, nappy care, etc.) were sorted into folders for each child. Parents receive this file when child moves to another room or leaves.

- Previous week's programme was evaluated.
- Developmental records updated from joint observation notes. (This information is used as a basis for parent interviews.)
- Action plan developed from issues.
- Weekly programme developed from action plans.
- Weekly programme displayed on wall for parents to see.

Attended staff meeting 6 p.m.–7.45p.m. (Pizzas ordered in!) Cathy chaired it. The agenda had been on view in the staff room.

Health issues: medical supplies to be ordered ... ice packs, digital thermometers. Staff asked questions re. – sterilization of thermometers, putting babies down on backs.
Workplace health and safety issues: Video on back safety available for staff to view at home. Safety Officer to visit. The Health Handbook for parents is to be updated – staff asked for suggestions. New medication forms to be developed.
Enrolments: Parents to be reminded that forms are due in for next year. Start to 'graduate' toddlers to D's group from November, rather than all at once after the Christmas break. Comments indicated that staff felt older children's visits with younger children were working well. Discussed ideas for rainy days ... set up one room with climbing equipment, use staff area as TV room, share morning tea (e.g., older children with toddlers).
Professional development: Forms to fill in re. goals/needs for profes-sional development ... where staff want to be in five years' time. Cathy discussed orientation of new staff members. Was anyone interested in being a mentor? Discussed sharing of resources and articles.
Parent subcommittee: Staff member who attends this committee re-ported on meeting. Plans for staff Christmas function are in hand.
General business: Two staff members shared their thoughts on trans-itions – from home to centre as well as the transitions within the centre. This led to an interesting discussion about children having choice. Some staff saw the benefits of choice in terms of greater contentment and less conflict for children. The group felt that the centre atmosphere was much more positive. They had come a long way in a short time.

I was impressed with the climate of the meeting. There was lots of laughter and a good feeling as the staff shared the pizzas and the discussion. I also noticed that matters raised at the meeting were followed up the next day.

These brief observations helped Bronwyn build her understanding of the many facets that are a part of the director's role. In discussing them with me when I visited, Bronwyn also recalled another incident from a previous teaching practice in a day-care setting which had highlighted the skills a director needed in order to lead a professional staff as well as build cooperation with parents. She said:

> It was early one morning and both the director and I were busy setting up when I heard the gate open and clang shut. I heard the director say in a surprised voice, 'Is it 7.30 already?' . . . and a male voice saying, 'No. It's only a quarter past seven.'
>
> As I looked out of my room I saw the director welcome the toddler and his dad and heard her say, 'Take him to his room and play with him there. The staff are not on duty until 7.30 . . . that's when the centre officially opens . . . but you're welcome to play with him in the room until then.'

Bronwyn said that this incident had not only aroused her admiration for the director's communication skills, but had also helped her come to realize the many people who needed to be considered in the day-care situation. She said that in doing her best for children and families she had not previously thought about the rights of colleagues. This incident, however, had made her think about the need for reasonable cooperation between the adults in children's lives. She said:

> This director's actions showed me that if parents expect staff to do their job properly . . . then parents have to cooperate too. If the centre's hours are clearly stated . . . and they were . . . then parents should accept them. In this case . . . I saw that the child enjoyed a special time with his dad and the director safeguarded the staff's preparation time . . . which they really needed. This meant that the staff didn't feel resentful or that they'd been taken for granted.

By reflecting on her observations of the ways in which these directors carried out their roles, Bronwyn became more aware of the need to consider the perspectives of all the adults and children associated with a centre. This involved the director in recognizing and considering competing needs, as well as deciding on what was reasonable in terms of cooperation and expectations for all parties. These decisions then had to be communicated in ways that helped those concerned to accept and appreciate the reasons for the decision. From her range of teaching practice experiences Bronwyn was able to see that the larger the staff and parent body, the more complex this task becomes for the director or principal. The building of relationships among colleagues can also be more difficult where there are many members of staff.

Braving the staff room

In large institutions such as primary schools, the staff room often takes on a life of its own. It can become an 'institution' within the institution. Spending time in the staff room is often anticipated with some fear and dread by student teachers. Sherrin wrote:

Prior to this prac I found staff rooms to be stressful places that made me feel uncomfortable. My peers did too. We talked about their special type of infrastructure which makes a newcomer stand out or feel foolish, particularly if you attempt to sit on the one spare chair which unbeknownst to you is 'owned' by the Year Seven teacher. Our shared experiences suggested that, as student teachers, we were either pressured to conform to the staff-room community and its entangled web of rules or were segregated, making us feel that we had some social disease. In talking with other students I found I was not the only one to manufacture all kinds of reasons to stay in my classroom and thereby avoid the staff room.

But after this last prac my fears of staff rooms have diminished. Instead of counting down the minutes until I could leave the staff room I was counting the minutes until I could get there. Thanks to a mixed bunch of zany, fun-loving people I was able to rise to the challenge of the staff room. My practicum was at a school in the country where the staff room was warm and cosy and everyone sat around one table. Although at first I was apprehensive of its intimate nature, the small staff room made it easier to get to know everyone. All the staff made me feel welcome and included me in conversations. I now feel more empowered and more able to cope with the whole staff-room ex-perience. I am amazed at how one warm fuzzy experience can wipe out so many black spots.

In talking with Sherrin's tutorial group about their staff-room experiences after their teaching practice there was general consensus that students could be better prepared for some of the staff-room realities. Although many students had had positive experiences, all agreed that they put on a brave front when they initially entered the staff room. Samantha-Lee recounted how on her first morning in the staff room her supervising teacher had tapped on a glass to obtain everyone's attention. Samantha-Lee said:

My throat felt like sandpaper and I could feel my palms getting sweaty. She announced my arrival and status to the sea of faces ... and then I was expected to say something. All I can remember saying is, 'If you have any hints, tips or advice, I'm all ears.' It felt like one of my worst moments ... but it proved to be very worthwhile. I guess because they knew who I was, staff started conversations ... and they shared many of their teaching stories ... and gave me some great advice.

Other suggestions made by the students to overcome staff-room fears were:

- to share some of your initial anxieties with your supervising teacher and ask if there is someone who could 'show you the ropes' or help you through the first morning tea or lunch break;

- to make the effort to go to the staff room frequently, and not hide in your classroom, so that others will come to see you as 'a regular';
- to contribute to the conversation if opportunities arise, or create an opportunity for conversation by sharing an experience;
- to join in other aspects of school life so that you get to know other teachers in their work context and have a common base for discussion in the staff room;
- to sit in different areas of the staff room from time to time so that you have a chance to talk with different members of staff;
- to make the most of the occasions when you are feeling isolated and alone by observing the informal networks among the staff and seeking to discover ways of joining the networks.

All these suggestions involve effort on your part. Most students agreed that when they had been 'brave' and had shown a positive, friendly attitude, and a willingness to contribute and communicate, they had found teachers in the staff room who were prepared to reciprocate.

Collaborating with colleagues

The term 'collaboration' is sometimes used in a way that suggests that it is a natural phenomenon and that schools or centres are, by their organizational nature, collaborative enterprises. Nothing could be further from the truth! Only those who have worked towards achieving meaningful collaboration with other teachers understand the effort needed. Many skills and abilities are required in order to collaborate – giving and receiving advice, offering and accepting support, and providing and benefitting from feedback and criticism ('Guidelines for preparation of early childhood professionals' 1996). Although these skills may seem relatively simple, as Luke and Ben discovered from their teaching practice experiences, acquiring them is not as easy as it first appears. Luke and Ben had two very different experiences of collaborating with colleagues.

Luke and another student from a different teacher education institute were undertaking their teaching practice in an environmental education centre. Because this centre catered for children of primary school age who camped at the site and explored the surrounding outdoor environment through a range of activities, a relaxed, holiday atmosphere prevailed. For Luke and the other student, however, the atmosphere between them was anything but relaxed because they found their opinions about how to approach situations clashing. Luke gave this example:

> As I was to read a story to the class I spoke to the children and told them to make themselves comfortable. I reminded them that if they wanted to see the pictures, they would need to sit up the front. Many of the children lay on the floor, some leaned against the wall and others sat

at the front. I was just about to begin the story when the other student walked in and told the children to sit up, move to the front and cross their legs, which they did – but the relaxed informal atmosphere was gone. I did not want to confuse the children so continued with the story, but later I approached the student to talk about what had happened. I was promptly told that I obviously didn't know what I was doing. I wished to talk about this some more, but the other person did not. This infuriated me and I decided that I did not want to work with this person further.

Upon reflection, Luke said he had realized that what had happened was not very professional. Ideally, they should have been able to talk about different approaches and respect, support, encourage and learn from each other. In talking with other teachers and peers about his experience Luke discovered two differing views. He wrote:

One group said that it is best to leave that sort of person in their own little world, while the other group suggested that everything should be able to be worked out – that we should be able to collaborate and work as a team. In future I would try to meet any similar situation with enthusiasm and make many attempts to rectify the difficulty. If no progress was being made and the situation didn't improve, though, I would not compromise the education of my students (or my stress levels) for such a person. As I thought further about this, I wondered why there are such differences in philosophies and teaching approaches. Some of my friends suggested that it may have more to do with personalities and that I may be egotistical when I say that I think I approached the situation correctly. I agree that we all have our own styles and attitudes; however, we all need to be able to work together and be prepared to give as well as take.

Luke was discovering some of the complexities associated with collaboration and professional partnerships. There is real skill required in giving and receiving feedback, particularly if the partners are coming from contrasting perspectives. Our own feelings, emotions and confidence levels all play a part in our ability to give and receive feedback and criticism. It is also inevitable that conflict and anger will result if a person's competence or values are challenged (Meade-Roberts et al., 1993). If dealt with, that anger can be used, as Luke discovered, to think further about the situation and to motivate change. Developing a collaborative relationship becomes almost impossible, however, if one party refuses to communicate. The lines of communication have to be kept open. Stacey (1991: 97–8) makes a number of suggestions for handling criticism which you may find helpful:

• Listen carefully so that you are clear about what is being said. Remember that criticism is opinion and may not necessarily be fact.

- Take several deep breaths before responding and then reply as honestly as you can. If the criticism is valid this may be difficult, but it is better to acknowledge it. You may want to explain your actions but don't offer excuses.
- If the criticism is untrue say so but be short and focused in your denial.
- Show that you take the criticism expressed seriously and that you want to talk about the matter further.
- Although it is important to recognize the feelings of all those concerned, 'focus on the facts of the problem rather than getting caught up in the emotion'.

Ben had a much more positive experience in collaboration when he was asked to contribute to a planning group discussion for the Family and Friends' Day to be held at the preschool. Ben described it this way:

This was the first time I felt on the same level as the other teachers. Because the day was to consist of activities that would involve the family and friends of the children, the planning was to focus on how these activities could be linked with the interests of the preschool children. A meeting time was arranged and we all sat around a table. I felt a little nervous even though I knew what I had planned and why. First we discussed the format – how things would happen, the rooms to be used, the set-up outdoors and how family and friends would be greeted. The discussion allowed everyone to speak. When I spoke, the teachers didn't look at me in a funny way or criticize what I had to say and that felt good.

Next we talked about the specific activities each teacher had planned and I talked about my planning. I found it great that we were talking about our planning using the same language so that everyone under-stood what was being said. Working with other teachers like this also gave me a sense of how close I am to finishing my degree and what skills I have and can use.

I learned several things from this experience. It gave me confidence knowing that I can work with other teachers as peers – that I'm not the odd one out. I also realized that I can discuss my planning and ideas with other teachers and that these are respected. This experience also made me think about the value of regular discussions between teachers because I learned such a lot from hearing other teachers' thinking and explanations of their planning.

By being able to participate in a collaborative process, Ben was able to experience the benefits of collaboration first hand. The fact that Ben's colleagues supported and valued his contribution gave his confidence a boost, which in turn enabled him to see the many benefits that can be derived when teachers are prepared to cooperate – to work in agreement with one another as well as collaborate – to share in the making of decisions as well as their implementation (Rodd, 1994). Some of you may be thinking that Ben's view of collaboration could have been very different if, like Luke, he had experienced negative feedback. Luke's and Ben's contrasting experiences highlight the importance of developing skill in giving and receiving feedback and criticism in a way that is beneficial to all parties. Maintaining effective communication, respecting the other's contribution and sharing in the decision-making process are essential if collaboration is to occur.

BUILDING COOPERATION WITH PARENTS

Building cooperation and collaboration between teachers and parents has been a priority in early childhood education for many years (Bredekamp, 1987; Ebbeck, 1991; Henry, 1996; Stacey, 1991). This is because teachers regard children's families as partners in the educational process. With young children so dependent on their families, parent support of the school and its programme is vital to the child's well-being and motivation, while the school's support and valuing of the child's home and culture is essential to the well-being of the family ('Guidelines for preparation of early childhood professionals', 1996).

If you are like most students entering teaching practice, from your studies you will recognize the importance of the parent–teacher relationship and be keen to develop your own skills in this regard. There is a need to think carefully, however, about what you need to know about the development of these relationships, the particular skills you need to develop and what you can reasonably do in your particular setting.

What's involved in developing effective parent–teacher relationships?

From your readings and observations you will know that there are many practical steps a teacher can take to promote the parent–teacher relationship. For instance, in getting to know parents, teachers can gauge each parent's particular interests and comfort level in being involved in their children's education. On this basis many different types of involvment might be offered. For example, some parents may be happy participating in classroom activities and working with children. Others may prefer to contribute to committees or fund-raising efforts, while others may want advice and support in child rearing or social contact with other parents.

Thinking about ways of gathering information from parents and giving information to parents about their child and aspects of the programme is also important. For instance, is this done in formal ways such as through interviews, reports and newsletters, or is this done using far more informal means? Are various two-way communication processes used? Is the teacher

Plate 6.2 There are many ways in which parents support their child's education. Some are happy to participate in classroom activities. (Photo courtesy of Northgate State Primary School.)

available for a chat with a parent at arrival or departure times? Are there opportunities to request a meeting? Is use made of telephone conversations or a parent–teacher notebook for parents who have have difficulty getting to the centre frequently? Considering strategies for meeting the needs of parents is also an important aspect. For instance, do parents see the centre as a source for social contact with other people, or are they so preoccupied with other aspects of their lives that they have little time to spend at the centre?

If you are aware that factors such as these can influence the way in which a teach goes about developing parent–teacher relationships you will more readily understand that the type of parent involvement will differ in different centres. As you gain experience in different teaching practice settings you will have opportunities to observe and participate in various approaches to parent involvement. In fact, observing the ways in which your supervising teacher communicates with parents and talking with your teacher about why particular strategies are used or particular emphases are placed on particular activities can be extremely useful in developing your understanding of that particular teacher's goals for the parent–teacher relationship.

What skills can be developed for communicating with parents?

For many supervising teachers, finding ways to help students develop their practical skills in working with parents poses some difficulties. There are a number of reasons for this. If the duration of teaching practice is only three or four weeks, then there is really not enough time for students to come to know parents well or to develop a relationship. It is also important that students do not do anything that might damage the relationship that may only just be developing between a parent and teacher. Gay, an experienced supervising teacher, expressed her thoughts this way:

> I've found that a lot of students don't quite know what to do in relation to parents. Some will have a little chat with them because they feel they should ... but a few students I've had have wanted to become best friends with parents in a hurry ... and that really bothers me ... and I find it a difficult situation to deal with. I realized I couldn't say, 'I really don't want you to become too friendly with parents' ... because I really haven't got anything to hide ... but when I thought about it some more, I realized I was worried about how the parents might interpret what the student said about their child. It takes a long time to get to know children ... and parents ... and you have to have the really big picture ... and I don't think a student teacher ... or anyone ... can get that in just a few weeks.'

Against the background of the types of concerns raised by Gay I talked further with supervising teachers and students about the kinds of experiences students could undertake during teaching practice to develop their skills in communicating effectively with parents. Both teachers and students agreed that it was vital that before teaching practice began the students should discuss their goals and ideas for developing these particular skills with their teachers. The teachers in turn needed to outline their own approach to working with parents and discuss how realistic the students' goals might be for a particular setting. Once the goals had been clarified and agreed to, the teachers were in a better position to support the students and provide opportunities in which the goals could be pursued, while the students were more confident because they knew they were working within the parameters of the teachers' expectations.

Goals for developing communication skills

Some of the goals that it was agreed that students could pursue in most early childhood settings included:

- to observe the teacher's style of communication with parents, the strategies used and the activities emphasized – and to discuss these observations with the teacher;

147

- to introduce yourself to parents – through an introductory poster, a note sent home or a social conversation with individual parents;
- to get to know parents by being available to talk with them at the beginning or end of sessions – a general comment about the day or about something a child enjoyed doing was seen to be a useful 'opener';
- to listen to what parents have to say – informally seek their views on topical issues;
- to join in activities designed to foster family participation – such as grandparents' day – a fathers' night – a sausage sizzle for all the family;
- to chat with parents who may be visiting or on roster and help them feel at ease;
- to explain how parents could participate or assist in an activity or routine;
- to invite a parent to contribute to the programme (e.g., play a musical instrument, bath a baby, make bread or pasta);
- to make posters or create displays for the notice board that communicate information to parents;
- to write a newsletter or send home a note about 'our' week at the school or centre – children can be encouraged to contribute to these newsletters with comments or drawings;
- to attend meetings organized for parents if appropriate;
- to participate in a parent meeting by sharing information or contributing to a discussion on a particular topic;
- to communicate with families through children by having the children make invitations or write thank-you notes;
- to thank parents personally for their participation in events or for their contribution to the programme.

Korina had the opportunity to develop many of these practical skills during her last teaching practice. She wrote:

> With each of my pracs the interaction I have had with parents has gradually increased as I have become more confident. As I began to believe in myself as a 'teacher', the roles I carried out became more like those of a teacher. I casually talked with parents about their child and what they had done that day. If certain resources were needed for an activity later in the week, then, with the teacher's permission, I wrote a note home to parents asking for their cooperation. I was still hesitant in approaching parents, though, and I must admit that most of the spontaneous conversations with parents were initiated by them.
>
> Before my last prac I shared with my supervising teacher my need for more experience in interacting with parents and she gave me lots of opportunities. During the weeks I was 'in control' I greeted children and parents at the door. Some children were a little confused by this, and I had to reassure them that their teacher was inside the room. Most parents were open and friendly and made me feel more confident and

comfortable. Because they knew I was a student, however, they still went to the teacher with any 'real' issues. Where appropriate, the teacher referred them back to me so that I had to deal with the information that Uncle Tom was picking David up instead of his Mum or make a decision about whether Sally could bring her new dog to show the children. I enjoyed this responsibility and I found my personal philosophy coming into play. For example, if I believed having a pet at preschool was unhygienic, I would have explained to Sally's Mum that it wouldn't be appropriate for Sally to bring her dog. Because the children had set up a vet's surgery in their play, however, I thought it would be a valuable experience for Sally to share how she looked after her dog Tex.

My teacher also thought it would be a good experience for me to organize the excursion. Although she was ultimately in control, I took most of the responsibility. I wrote and sent a reminder home about the excursion details. I found it easier to communicate through the written rather than the spoken word, and realized I would probably choose to write messages home when I am teaching. I recognize that this approach could be impersonal and that parents need other forms of communication as well. I also wrote a reminder note beside the sign – in book in case the note home was not read. On the excursion day I had to allocate a child and a friend to each adult and explain the adults' responsibilities. It was a great experience because I had to 'perform' in front of seventeen adults who all had their eyes on me.

My experiences this prac have shown me that it is essential to be outgoing and approachable and that not all parents will approach me first. I also saw the value of using a variety of communication strategies because it increases the chance of the message being received by parents.

Korina was fortunate that she was in a situation where her teacher felt comfortable for her to have as much contact with parents as she did. In Korina's situation the parents recognized that any 'real' issues were to be discussed with the teacher, and the teacher was able to decide whether they were appropriate for Korina to handle. This meant that the teacher knew what Korina was talking with parents about and felt comfortable with how Korina would respond. Korina also knew that she must refer the parents to the teacher if they did want detailed information about their child.

Lana had a somewhat different experience with parents. There was little parent participation in the preschool where Lana was, although her supervising teacher was quite happy for Lana to invite parents to participate. As Mother's Day was approaching, Lana suggested that the children invite their mothers to an afternoon tea. The children made the invitations, and on the day helped set the tables and make the scones. In spite of her best efforts to run ahead of schedule during the day, Lana found that by rest time they were behind time and the children were over-excited. Lana wrote:

Although we were behind time things were generally going to plan. The mothers arrived and the children gave them their scones. Then Jesse and two other boys remembered they each had a lollipop in their bag. This had been Brenton's gift to everyone, as he had turned 5 that day. We had agreed that the children would put their lollipops in their bags and eat them when they got home. Jesse kept asking me if he could eat his lollipop now. His mother watched me as I said 'No', and reminded him of what we had decided to do that morning. Jesse then began to be difficult and nagged his mother, who said he could go and get his lollipop. Within a few minutes most of the children had their lollipops. All I could do was turn a blind eye.

In talking with the children about the afternoon, we had said that they could be with their Mums or they could play with puzzles or listen to stories on the carpet where the aide would be sitting. After about five minutes, the five children who had been on the carpet began to run around the room excitedly. I wanted to redirect them but didn't want to sound like an ogre. Nor did I want to look like I was incapable of controlling the children. (I found this a difficult situation. When the parent is there, who is responsible for controlling the child?) When Jesse climbed on the oven in home corner and jumped off and was about to repeat the performance I felt I had to step in, even though his mother was standing nearby talking to another Mum, but watching him. I asked Jesse to come and sit on the carpet with me until he calmed down and then I told him he was to sit next to his mother.

I learned a lot from this afternoon's experience. I learned that although children need to be made aware of a change in the routine, it is important not to make too big a deal of it. I felt I may have over-excited a few children, who in turn found it difficult to rest and then were over-tired and reacted differently. I also realized that the environment could have been set up more effectively. With an additional table of fun activities there would have been more to occupy the children. I also learned that it is essential to sit down and involve the children in creating the rules for a special event such as this, so they know what to do and what behaviour is expected of them. I believe that children are sometimes confused by the fact that different behaviours are accepted at home compared with those required at preschool. While one set of rules may not be better than another, just different, children need to be aware of this distinction. This distinction must become very blurred for them when parents and teachers are together.

In spite of my hassles, the parents really enjoyed their afternoon. They said they had enjoyed socializing with other Mums and their special time with their child. It reinforced for me that it is worthwhile to have parents sharing in positive fun events with children whenever possible.

Lana's account of her venture into parent participation is a valuable reminder that it requires a great deal of effort on the part of the teacher. Not only does it require organization and planning, but also all your teaching and communicative skills as you interact with children and their parents in situations where roles become somewhat blurred for all participants. If this blurring can be used constructively, however, to challenge stereotypes of 'them' (the parents) and 'us' (the teachers), and bring parents into a more open and equal partnership with teachers in the educational process, then the children and their families and the teacher and the school will gain strength from the support of the other. This is why it is so important to build cooperation with parents. Developing skills in learning to communicate effectively with parents is only one step in this dynamic and complex process. It is nevertheless an essential one.

SUMMARY

In order to be an effective teacher you not only have to develop trusting relationships with children, you also have to develop working relationships with adults. Your teaching practice experiences can enable you:

- to develop and refine your skills in building working relationships with your supervising teacher and other colleagues;
- to become familiar with a range of formal and informal organizational structures and the ways in which they influence relationships;
- to observe how adults work as members of a team;
- to see how effective parent–teacher relationships can be built;
- to gain skills and confidence in communicating with parents.

In developing your relationship with your supervising teacher it is important to consider how best to communicate so that you can achieve your goals. Being open and honest in sharing your thinking, being prepared to talk about your perceptions or difficulties and seeking specific information and guidance will help your supervising teacher understand your reality and assist your teacher to focus responses and provide opportunities that are most likely to meet your needs. Having a positive, enthusiastic attitude and demonstrating that you are open minded and ready to learn also contribute to effective working relationships with colleagues.

These same communication skills and enthusiastic attitudes will help you begin to build relationships with parents. If your teaching practice is of short duration, the development of collaborative relationships may not be a realistic aim. Nevertheless, you may have the opportunity to observe such collaboration in action and to identify the factors that contribute to its achievement. Children and their families as well as teachers benefit when effective relationships are established.

SUGGESTED ACTIVITIES

- Imagine that you are a supervising teacher. What characteristics would your ideal student have? List them. Discuss and compare your list with another student. Think about what you could do to develop some of those ideal student characteristics.

- In a small group, share experiences you have had in developing relationships with supervising teachers. If they have been positive ones, list down the things you and your teacher did that promoted their success. If there were difficulties in the relationship, try to identify their causes and discuss some strategies that you might use to overcome them if faced with a similar situation in the future.

- Describe to a friend the formal organization of a school or centre with which you are familiar. Outline the roles you perceive to be taken by people occupying particular positions. (If you are describing the setting where you are undertaking teaching practice, you may be able to check out your perceptions with the people concerned.) Discuss how you see the form of organization contributing to the functioning of the school or centre.

- Imagine you are working in a team-teaching situation. Your colleague wants to give the children rewards (jelly beans, gold stars and stamps) when they achieve at a high standard. You want to foster the child's sense of achievement and satisfaction without offering external rewards. Role play the discussion that you would have in order to negotiate some workable arrangement that you could both 'live' with. Have an observer make notes of your discussion and provide you with feedback concerning your skills in communication and negotiation.

- List what you think parents of young children might be interested to know about their child's experiences at preschool or school. After you have done this, talk with as many parents of young children as you can – preferably parents not associated with your teaching practice setting. Try to find out what parents want to know about their child's education, what their experiences with early education have been, the concerns they may have, and their suggestions for developing effective relationships with teachers. Compare the parents' views with your own ideas and note any similarities and differences. In the light of the information gathered from parents and your own knowedge of early childhood settings and the teacher's role, formulate some goals for developing cooperation between parents and teachers.

7

MAKING THE MOST OF THE TEACHING PRACTICE EXPERIENCE

In this chapter we will consider a number of students' stories which provide some insights into ways in which you can make the most of your teaching practice experience. Actions that contribute to your learning during teaching practice include:

- the setting of personal goals;
- developing and testing out ways to achieve those goals;
- reflecting on the teaching experiences that result.

THE SETTING OF PERSONAL GOALS

Throughout this book emphasis has been given to the fact that learning to teach is a very personal process. As you talk with peers about teaching practice you will find that you each have had different experiences. This is because in undertaking teaching practice you are drawing on your own unique past experiences as well as your current understanding of specialized knowledge. Your teaching practice is also being influenced by your particular setting as well as your own expectations, learning style and personality. Because learning to teach is such an individual process, you will find it valuable to set yourself some personal goals to achieve during your teaching practice. These goals are likely to be in addition to those set as part of the course requirements.

Recently I worked with a group of student teachers who undertook some personal goal setting before their teaching practice. As a framework for our thinking we used a report by the Queensland Board of Teacher Registration (Hobart *et al.*, 1994), in which beginning teachers identified four knowledge sources they drew upon most in their first year of teaching. These sources were:

- knowledge about self (the person I am);
- knowledge about children;
- knowledge about communicating;
- knowledge about the practice of teaching.

After considering the beginning teachers' experiences outlined in this report, the students began to examine their own knowledge in these areas. For many students this examination was more than just a cursory exercise, as it included identifying and accepting personal weaknesses and strengths. For instance, Melissa wrote:

> I believe my main strengths lie in my ability to interact effectively with children. My weakness is that I am not such a successful interactor with adults in school settings. How I communicate and relate to others is very much an aspect of my personality. I see myself as one who views and observes, and when I feel confident and comfortable I will become a contributing participant. This type of behaviour is something which has to be changed in order for me to be a successful teacher.

Tania, on the other hand, felt at ease with adults but not so confident in communicating with children. Tania wrote:

> As I am fairly outgoing, I am confident about the way I communicate with most adults. I do, however, experience a little difficulty getting my message across to children. The challenge I face this prac, which is in a preschool, is conveying my messages to this younger age group in a way they will understand. By the time I finish explaining what I mean I have lost their attention. I thought it was just a matter of finding smaller words . . . but I'm not sure if that's the problem. I need to think more about why I'm losing them.

As Melissa's and Tania's comments show, their goals were derived from an honest appraisal of themselves, and their own knowledge and abilities. By thinking about their current understanding and practice, *they* were making some decisions about *their* actions. After identifying their goals these students had to work out ways of achieving them. Many said they found this a harder task than identifying the goals, but they agreed it was an essential process if their goals were to be achieved. In the stories which follow seven students tell of their experiences in seeking to achieve their goals.

STORIES STEMMING FROM SETTING GOALS

There are many aspects to think about as you read these stories. You may find yourself identifying with a particular goal or story because of your personal experiences, or you may gain new knowledge or insight as another student's reflection suggests a notion you had not previously considered. You may find it useful to use a particular story as a discussion starter with a group of peers, or you may want to jot down your own experiences relating to a similar situation and compare notes. Above all, it is hoped that you will gain a sense of camaraderie as you read these stories of fellow students and realize that, in seeking to achieve your goals, you have to act with a purpose in mind, be prepared to use relevant strategies, and to reflect honestly on your actions and their consequences.

Kylie's story – thinking further about my values and their influences

In deciding on her particular goal, Kylie wrote:

> I have a strong belief that children should learn to respect each other. This gives everyone the right to learn in a safe environment. Personal values such as this one play a significant part in my decision making in the classroom, and I see some of my success as a teacher in terms of whether the children demonstrate some of my personal values – as well as show progress academically. In the brief time on prac it is difficult to judge whether children are absorbing my personal values. Nevertheless, I will use this short period to clarify further my thinking about values, and their influence on teachers' actions and children's experiences.

As Kylie got to know her teaching practice setting, which was a multi-age class for 6–8-year-olds, she realized that she would have an opportunity to see whether her personal value of 'showing respect for each other' could have some influence in the classroom. She wrote:

> I noted that Michael, a 7-year-old, was having difficulties with all his academic work except handwriting. Throughout the day it was common for many children to ostracize him, and say, 'I don't want to be in Michael's group. He's too slow.' Consequently Michael's confidence and self-esteem were very low. He would make remarks such as 'I can't do anything', and sit at his desk for long periods of time, fiddling with pencils but doing very little work.
>
> I decided to try to help him gain some self-confidence, using some of the strategies I had read about. I made an effort to acknowledge any ideas or comments that Michael contributed in class, and, when appropriate, repeated his suggestion to the entire class. Sometimes we were able to carry out his ideas. Initially some of the children were sarcastic towards Michael and his views. I had to make it clear to the class why it was important to respect each other and that I would not tolerate such remarks or sneers about other people's ideas. The children quickly realized that this was an issue I felt strongly about. Consequently, over the next few weeks derogatory remarks weren't verbalized as frequently and Michael was more willing to express his thoughts in class.
>
> To help Michael's self-esteem I also decided to work with his positive abilities. Because his handwriting was relatively good I asked him, in a quiet, one-to-one chat, if he could help me with my handwriting. Initially he was doubtful as to whether I was serious, but I convinced

him that I really did have difficulty doing cursive writing on the blackboard. We mutually decided when these 'lessons' were to take place, how he was going to teach me and what materials we would need. Every morning before school for the next two weeks he would find me and ask me to write out words and sentences. We laughed together about how terrible many of my letters were. Michael gave me positive feedback when my letter formations were improving. He took responsibility for finding another person to teach me when he was going to be away for a day and he even initiated helping other children during handwriting sessions. His mother came to school one morning and thanked me for taking time with him. She said she had never seen him so motivated to do his homework.

In reflecting on her experiences Kylie wrote:

> I was amazed at the effect that a little support, interaction and faith in a child's abilities could have. I realize that to form such a rapport with every child would be impossible. Nevertheless this experience has shown me that I can make a difference in a child's life if I take the time to recognize and respond to a child's unique abilities and needs. I also saw how the respect I showed for Michael, as well as all the other children, was beginning to have an influence on the behaviour of all the children in the class.

Kylie's reflections suggest that through this experience she became more aware of the ways in which her own particular values, combined with her knowledge of a child's need for self-confidence, influenced her teaching actions, and in turn, the children's experiences. She found that when she showed the children that she valued their ideas and opinions, they began to do the same for the other children in the class. In a classroom climate of sincerity and openness, the children were able to experience the building of mutual respect.

Bronwyn's story – moving beyond interactions to building relationships

Because Bronwyn was undertaking her teaching practice in the babies' and toddlers' group of a long day-care setting she knew that the quality of her relationships with the children and their parents were important. In thinking about the nature of her interactions she wrote:

> Although I have found interacting with children to have been one of the most satisfying aspects of past teaching practice experiences, I would like to move beyond 'interactions' to 'building relationships'. For me interaction implies the mutual engagement of two parties – that something is happening. Interactions are a state of doing. Relationships,

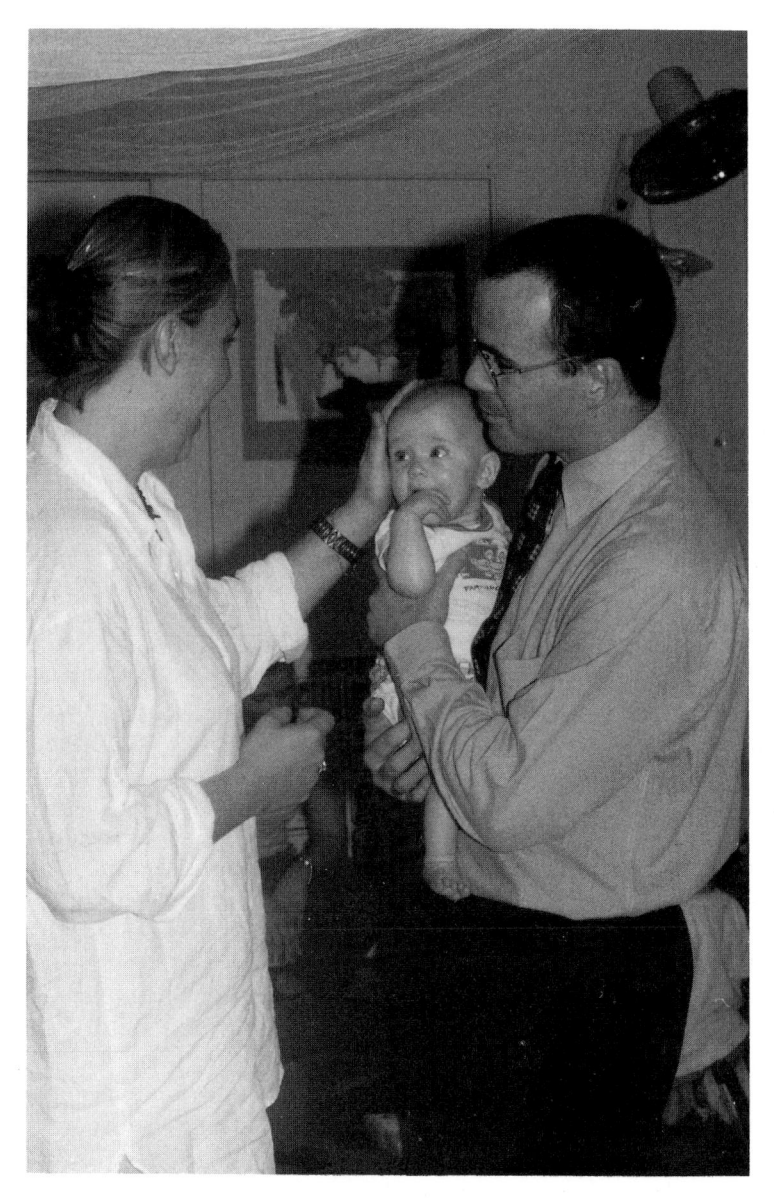

Plate 7.1 Building caring relationships involves positive interactions with children and their parents. (Photo courtesy of Lady Gowrie Child Centre, Brisbane.)

on the other hand, are a state of being. They refer to the connection, or tie, that exists between two persons. I want to enter into a caring relationship with each child which will enable me to understand each child better and consequently foster holistic development.

Bronwyn began to think about how she would enter into caring relationships by reminding herself of the strategies likely to promote positive interactions with babies and toddlers. She also reviewed strategies for interacting with their parents. In her story she wrote:

I believe I was more successful in building caring relationships with the children than their parents, although I sensed a ready acceptance in those parents who saw that I had an effective relationship with their child. For instance, at the close of 9-month-old Ben's first visit he clambered from his mother's lap to mine. When she next brought him in she called, 'Where's *our* friend Bronwyn?'

In building relationships I was reminded of how important it is to be sensitive to how children feel at different times of the day. This was brought home as I tried to accommodate 18-month-old David's irritability after he had experienced an upsetting lunch and sleep routine. I also saw the value of seeking information on home child-rearing practices. Having noted that Anna's mother had said 'Twinkle, twinkle, little star' was Anna's favourite song, I used the melody to soothe her to sleep. My experience with the triplets reminded me how differences in temperaments can influence relationships, with Yvette being reserved, Caitlin placidly accepting, while Izabella reached out to me at our first meeting.

I also became aware that there is a reverse side to relationships. Kathryn (13 months) arrived as an emergency enrolment early in my time at the centre. A medical crisis had turned life upside down for her out-of-town parents. There was an instant rapport between myself and her parents, and, as Kathryn was not accustomed to other staff members she became my responsibility. Although she initially explored the playground with glee, separation anxiety set in on her second visit, and, on this and subsequent occasions, she looked to me for comfort. Her father's course of treatment was extended, and it became apparent that I would be leaving the centre before Kathryn. This meant she had to adjust to yet another change during a difficult period in the life of her family. I realized the importance of looking at all aspects of a situation and not relying on rapport alone in deciding what is best for a child.

In reflecting on her experiences in building relationships, Bronwyn said that her placement in a day-care centre which provided for children on a regular as well as an occasional basis had convinced her that, in order to be responsive to family needs, the provision of occasional care was important.

She wondered, however, whether at a personal level she was suited to this task. She asked:

> Am I sufficiently dedicated and patient to soothe and support children continually as they separate and settle into a new environment? I found the constant changes to be my greatest challenge. The dynamics of the group are not only changing day to day, but also during the day. When David awoke from a nap he could have lost or gained several playmates. Am I adventurous and energetic enough to relish each day being on an uncharted sea? Am I perceptive enough to discern a child's interests and needs quickly, and sufficiently organized to provide appropriate resources and activities so that the children's time in care also has a clear educational benefit?

In reflecting on her experiences in building relationships with parents and children, Bronwyn became more aware of the characteristics of day-care settings which impacted on those relationships and the demands and opportunities they placed on teachers. In the process she also began to think about her own suitability for working with children in that particular context and her abilities to meet those demands. The teaching practice had helped her to come to know herself better.

Monica's story – helping children deal with difficult behaviour

An aspect of Monica's teaching with which she felt less comfortable related to dealing with children with behaviour problems. This was because in her previous teaching practice experiences she had not been exposed to children with difficult behaviours. In deciding on her goal Monica wrote:

> From my pre-practicum visits I have learned of one particular 4-year-old who is causing difficulty for both staff and the children at my teaching practice centre. Because of my lack of experience I see this as a challenging opportunity to learn more about guiding children's behaviour. My specific goal is to reduce the amount of disruption and physical and emotional upset caused to other children by children with behavioural problems.

To help herself to achieve this goal Monica had decided to read further on the topic, and be prepared with some strategies so that she could try to reduce the disruption and upset that Jason was causing. She wrote:

> From what I had been told about Jason I must admit that I had some preconceptions of him even though I didn't know him. After researching the topic I realized I needed to *develop a positive attitude towards him* if I was going to help him. It gave me confidence to know that I had gathered a number of strategies I could try in order to interact with him

positively. At the beginning of my first morning at the centre I heard a terrific yell. When I went to investigate the problem, Alex was crying and told me that Jason had hit him over the head with one of the trucks. When I asked Jason if this was true, he yelled, 'But he was annoying me and I wanted the truck.'

In this situation I was able to use one of my strategies, which was *to encourage Jason to use his words to express how he felt, rather than using physical force.* I explained to Jason that words can let people know how we feel and that it is better to use words rather than hurt people. I encouraged Jason to talk about what had happened but he was very uptight and found this difficult. I continued with this strategy, however, speaking to him individually and using a calm, soft voice until he began to relax. I talked about the consequences that would follow if he went on hurting other people. The next day Jason seemed to want to test me out. In one specific incident, after talking about the behaviour that was expected and the consequences which would result if he chose not to do as he was asked, Jason hit Aaron over the head with a book. I acted immediately and withdrew Jason from the situation. I told him that when he felt he could act properly we could talk and he could rejoin the group, but until then he was to remain by himself sitting on the step.

I also became aware of the need *to remind Jason of the rules ahead of time.* For instance, I found that it helped when I said, 'When you have tidied up your area, please sit on the cushions for story time.' If I did not give this reminder Jason got very distracted and confused about what to do next and often lashed out, whereas knowing what was expected of him seemed to minimize his aggression. Similarly, I could not say, 'Tidy up time', and expect Jason to tidy up on his own initiative as many of the other children were able to do. I found, however, that if I allocated specific jobs to all the children this worked well, and that with some encouragement and supervision Jason could fulfil this responsibility. I also realized how helpful it was *to give Jason positive feedback.* I'd say, 'It was great you helped John take the ladder to the shed. Now we've packed up we can have our special snack.' On these occasions it seemed as if he did want to please.

In reflecting on her experiences, Monica said:

I learned an incredible amount from my experience with Jason. I had a real purpose for my readings and reasons to seek out strategies. In building my relationship with Jason I became aware of just how different each child is. Even though textbooks suggest particular strategies, I had to discover just how Jason would respond to my particular ways of using them. I saw that getting to know Jason by observing and talking with him had to be a priority if I was to come to know his reasoning and understand how I could help him. Although I was only at the centre three weeks I feel I did get to know him and was able to help him reduce his negative behaviour.

This experience sparked some more questions for me. I wondered whether it would help if parents and teachers used the same types of discipline strategies and how a more consistent approach could be established: I realized that I need to seek advice about how to approach parents to talk about the difficulties their child might be having. I also decided I needed to find out about agencies or resource staff who can assist teachers and parents in such situations. Another issue I felt that I hadn't resolved related to how to provide for the other children in the group if my time is taken up with children like Jason.

Monica's reflections reveal the importance of doing your own thinking about your teaching actions. Although she was using recommended strategies, she had to discover how she herself put them into practice and what effect they would have on a particular child. The questions that were raised as part of her reflections were also important and provided her with a valuable framework for extending her understandings and skills in guiding behaviour.

Cindy's story – involving children in creating a unit of work

Cindy's reflections on her previous teaching practice experiences helped her to decide on her goals. She wrote:

In my previous prac in a primary school, I spent so much time planning my lessons and thinking about how I was going to manage the whole class that I didn't seem to get to know the children. Now I feel more confident about managing large groups and what I have to teach, I want to get to know the children as individuals and try to develop a unit of work in a way which involves the children in the process. I want the children to contribute their ideas for learning about a particular topic, and I would like to try a brainstorming strategy that I saw a teacher use to achieve this.

During a previous teaching practicum Cindy had seen a teacher using a brainstorming approach in which the children were invited to offer information on the topic, to indicate what they might like to know and do, and to suggest how they could find out more information. She felt this would be a useful means of helping her gain insights into the children's interests and prior knowledge, as well as involve them in planning a unit of work. Cindy described her experiences this way:

Prior to teaching practice I visited the Year Two classroom on several occasions. The environment was highly structured, with children sitting in rows of desks facing the blackboard which was filled with work. On no occasion did I see any group work, and lessons tended to be a series of individual tasks involving the completion of several worksheets. This impression was confirmed in a discussion with my teacher, who said she preferred a traditional approach which emphasized the development of the basic skills – reading, writing and mathematics. Furthermore, she told me that I was to use 'the dinosaur theme' as the focus for my continuous teaching period and requested that I have a unit outline and proposals ready before my prac started.

At first I felt thwarted in my plans to negotiate a curriculum with the children and nervous about planning, as I would have little chance to observe or get to know the children and would therefore have little idea of their needs, abilities and interests. After some consideration I decided that I could still negotiate the curriculum with the children in relation to the dinosaur theme. Because my teacher wanted me to have my lesson plans ready in advance, however, I realized I would have to explain to her that I wanted to involve the children in the process. After some discussion it was agreed that I could use the first three days of my first week to observe and get to know the children, and on Thursday morning conduct a brainstorming session with the children to establish their prior knowledge and interests in the topic. Based on this information I could then provide my teacher with my planning on the Friday.

The experience of negotiating with my teacher about what I wanted to do and why gave me insights into the process that must occur for teachers who have to work cooperatively in classrooms. I saw the need to express and discuss ideas and values so that they could be translated into workable arrangements that satisifed both parties.

During my observation days I took copious notes and gathered what information I could on the children's social, cognitive, physical and emotional development from what I saw them doing in the classroom and the playground. I was able to look at samples of their work and analyse their level of writing and mathematical understandings. As well, I engaged myself in conversation with them at every opportunity and gained some of their perceptions of their abilities. I also gathered what information I could from conversations with my teacher. The collection of these data in such a short time frame was tiring, but I wanted to establish as accurate an understanding as I could of each child.

Prior to the brainstorming session the supervising teacher and I had collected some resources from the library. I decided to display the books and charts in the room for the children to explore. They were very enthusiastic about the display and used any free time available to peruse the books. This proved to be a very effective way of engaging the children's interest for the forthcoming learning experiences. We also viewed a video on dinosaurs before the brainstorming session. In preparation for the session I divided a large sheet of paper into four sections:

- What do we already know about dinosaurs or the dinosaur age?
- What things would we like to know more about?
- How could we find out more about dinosaurs?
- Whom could we ask?

I was surprised by the response to this activity considering that the children had not previously engaged in this type of experience. The children were bursting to offer suggestions and to divulge facts, information and terminology that they already knew about. Furthermore, they were keen to offer lots of ideas for activities and were keen to bring in resources from home to assist our learning. This gave me considerable insight into the children's prior knowledge base which I feel I would not have achieved if I had not conducted this type of activity. Other unanticipated benefits from this activity were the links that were established between home and school. As children talked at home about their learning experiences, parents began to show interest in the classroom activities, with some providing more books, replicas and posters.

In reflecting on her experience, Cindy said:

I plan to continue to use this approach to curriculum development as I begin teaching next year, as it seems a means of ensuring that the planned learning experiences take into account the children's interests, prior knowledge and abilities. It also enables children to feel respected contributors to their own learning. Provided I also give full consideration to the syllabus guidelines as I use this approach, I feel that I will be able to provide children with meaningful learning experiences that not only reflect their input but also have the 'intellectual integrity' that is required.

Cindy had several personal goals: to involve children in creating the curriculum; to gain as much knowledge as she could about individual children; and to develop a unit of work using a particular technique. In the process of seeking to achieve these goals Cindy achieved many others: clarifying the reasons for her approach; negotiating with her supervising teacher; and establishing closer links with parents. Multiple learnings frequently follow from the setting of personally meaningful goals.

Susan's story – gaining confidence in speaking with adults

Susan indicated that deciding on her goal had been relatively easy. She wrote:

Feeling confident in talking to other teachers, administration staff and parents has always been an issue for me. I have often talked to friends and lecturers about ways in which I could build my confidence. It is not that I don't know how to do it or what to say. It is just that I am shy when I have to talk to people I don't know. Over the last one and a half years I have really tried to work on building my confidence with adults as I realize that a teacher must be able to communicate easily. My goal is to feel comfortable and confident as I speak with adults whom I don't know well.

Having decided upon this goal, Susan was rather taken aback when she found she had a male supervising teacher. She wrote:

I was delighted when I found I had been allocated a Year Two class, which was what I wanted, but my confidence took two steps back when I found out I had a male supervising teacher. This was really going to test my confidence as I had never worked with a male teacher before and I thought that there would be a different communication style. I decided that I still had to be confident and deal with everything in a professional way. As I got into the first week of prac I realized just how wrong my initial reactions had been. Having a male teacher was just like dealing with any new person in my life. He was a teacher, too, and had a lot to offer me as he was working on a mentoring programme. His goal for himself was to assist me to be as independent and self-reliant as possible.

I'm not sure whether he realized just how much he was helping me by setting this goal for himself. It really did help me to go one step further in my ability to communicate effectively with other teachers and parents within the school. The process began gradually, with John introducing me to everybody whom we came across. This was his way of showing me the ropes and making sure I knew who everybody was. Then it was up to me. Each day I would set myself little goals that I needed to accomplish. My diary looked like this:

Monday talk to Neil (teacher librarian) about resources for topic 'fairy tales'; check with John about cooking with the children.
Tuesday see deputy principal about the risk management policy in relation to cooking;
spend time in the staffroom at lunch;
book the Creative Skills Centre for art.

These goals helped me see what I was doing and that I was making progress. I became sufficiently confident to access resources from the library and storerooms without going to my supervising teacher first. I also invited the other Year Two teachers to watch a video that related to the topic we were doing and this resulted in more sharing of the resources between classrooms. With parents who came into the room before or after school, I would introduce myself and try to make some small talk. I found that everyone was very friendly and after the ice was broken they readily approached me at a later stage.

In reflecting on her experiences, Susan said:

> I felt my professionalism grow as my confidence with people grew. As I became confident in communicating with other teachers I found it easier to talk with parents and the administration staff in the school. As I begin teaching next year I will set myself similar goals and reach out to as many people as I can.

From this experience Susan found that success leads to more success, and that as she gained in confidence, contacts could be made more easily with other adults occupying a range of positions within the school setting. Susan knew that gaining this confidence in her own ability to communicate was important if she was to be effective as a beginning teacher.

Rachel's story – becoming organized and able to think on my feet

In deciding on her goals Rachel drew on her own assessments of her abilities in previous teaching practice experiences. She wrote:

> Last teaching practice I had the feeling that I was never quite 'organized'. This prac I want to improve my ability to organize the classroom, the children and myself. I want to be able to anticipate possible problems and find ways to prevent them arising. In short, I want to 'think on my feet' more effectively.

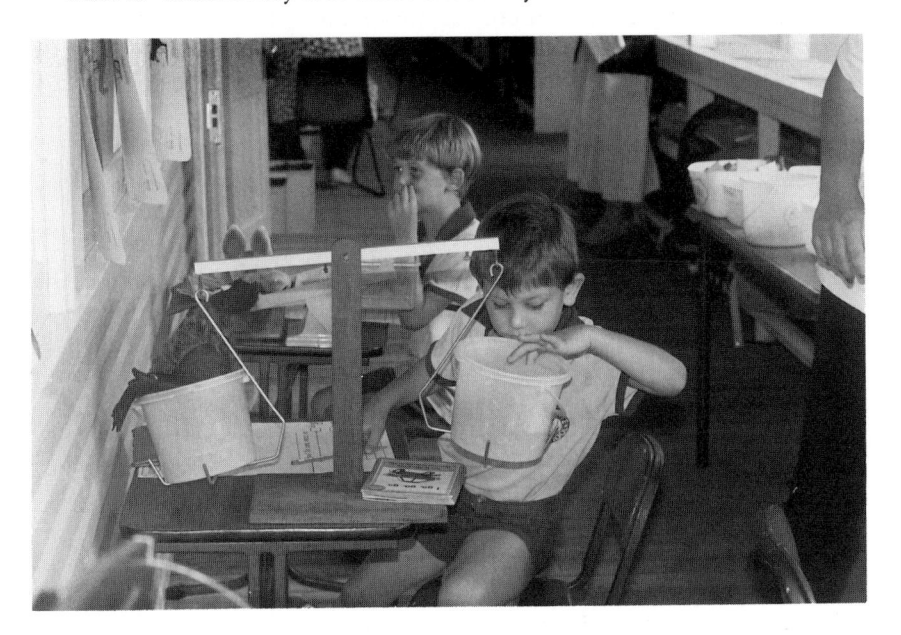

Plate 7.2 Ensuring that children understand what is expected of them is an important teaching strategy. (Photo courtesy of Northgate State Primary School.)

Although at first glance Rachel's goals might seem relatively easy to achieve, as you will see from Rachel's story they required her to consider many facets of her teaching in a Year One classroom. She wrote:

To help me achieve my goals I used a daily reflective diary and evaluated each day in terms of my organization of it. From the practical knowledge I gained I would work out a better way of organizing a situation so that I would be sure to learn from my mistakes. Here are some of the things I did, as well as some of the things I learned.

- I added a column to my daily programming sheet and in this wrote the things I needed to do and organize. I referred to this often and found it helped me to think ahead.
- I learned new strategies to ensure that the children understood my instructions and knew what to do. For example, after outlining their task I would ask, 'Now what is the first thing you will need to do?'
- I found that encouraging children to anticipate possible problems and come up with solutions was an effective means of organization. For instance, I would ask, 'What might happen if everyone decides to use the clay at the one time?' We would then together work out some guidelines that were likely to prevent the problem from arising.
- I discovered that even when you have thought ahead and prepared, things don't always go to plan and that you need to be flexible. Before class I had drawn lines on the board ready for a handwriting lesson but another teacher had rubbed them off during her lesson. I turned 'ruling the lines' into part of the lesson, asking the children to explain what lines I needed to draw and why – the head, body and tail lines.
- I found that transition games are just as popular in primary class-rooms as they are in preschool settings and can help avoid 'rushes'. At the same time they can be enjoyable learning experiences.
- I realized that I have a tendency to get caught up helping individual children. I learned to make sure that all the groups were working effectively before I began to work with individuals. I also recognized the need to share my time fairly so that I was not always working with the children who were struggling. I also had a responsibility to extend the children who were coping well.
- I became aware that it was important to assist children who had been absent to become familiar with what the class had done while they were away. It showed them they were valued and respected. This, however, required preparation and organization on my part.
- Organizing a classroom in ways that allow children to work at their own pace can be quite a challenge. Initially I had problems with children who finished quickly and others who needed more time. I had to make sure there was always some activity for children to engage in. I got lots of practice thinking on my feet filling in those last couple of minutes before the bell went.

- I came to recognize that reflection and sharing what has been learned are important aspects of the learning process for children as well as adults, and that it is important to allow time for this. Allowing time for 'tidy up' is also necessary if you are to avoid doing it yourself!
- Instead of trying to do everything myself I came to rely on the children's help – handing out books, being responsible for keeping their area tidy. I saw that this had benefits for them as well as me.
- I sought the advice and expertise of my supervising teacher as I talked through my ideas and plans and asked for feedback. I gained many insights from her experience about how to organize for learning, and she assisted me to put my plans into practice.
- I found that parents can offer great support and make organization easier by supervising small groups, listening to children read, and helping to make resources. I had the opportunity to work with parents more closely than I have ever done before and found that they helped me to achieve my goals.

In concluding her story, Rachel said:

> Reflecting daily on my organization and 'in-flight' thinking helped me to clarify what strategies were effective and what I could do in future situations. I felt my abilities developing as I took more responsibility for the class. This experience helped me discover the practical value of reflecting. I feel that I have not only achieved my goals but have also developed my reflective skill to the point that it will continue to foster my practical knowledge.

In reviewing aspects of organization each day, Rachel was able to identify areas that needed to be improved as well as strategies that worked well. It is interesting to note that, in reflecting on organization, Rachel was also reflecting on her ability to anticipate, prepare and be flexible, and to communicate her directions in ways that were understood. In addition, she was developing a teaching approach that catered for individuals as well as groups and that welcomed the contributions of children as well as parents. This is another example of the interconnectedness of the many facets of teaching.

Lynette's story – extending children's play in playful ways

In deciding upon her goal, Lynette said that she wanted to understand how, in a practical sense, she could 'teach' and extend young children's learning in the context of their play without taking the control away from the children. She wrote:

> Throughout my early childhood teacher education course emphasis has been given to basing planning on observations of children's interests

and developmental needs. I would like to build my knowledge and skill in doing this while at the same time fostering children's play. I want to explore how to have input into the play while still allowing children to retain ownership of their play.

In thinking about how to achieve this goal, Lynette listed some possible strategies she could try. These were:

- to develop my knowledge of children's interests and level of involvement in the play by observing and playing with them;
- to use questioning to encourage children to discuss what they are working on and how they plan to develop their play further;
- to provide extra materials or suggestions that could extend the play in the light of the knowledge gained;
- to keep the children's play structures in place if possible, to allow play to continue in the next session.

Lynette described her experiences in these terms:

From the start of my prac, 4-year-old Brendon's strong interest in mechanical things was evident. He spent most of his time in the block corner using large and small blocks to construct cars, boats and roads. He rarely ventured into areas where the painting, collage, drawing and writing activities were, and his only other apparent interest was the computer. Although he spent most of his time in the block area I noticed that his play seemed rather superficial. He would construct his car or boat, either by himself or in cooperation with others, and then very noisily drive it.

I started very slowly with Brendon, asking him what type of boat or car he had. His car was most definitely 'a Ferrari' and 'it goes very fast – 151 kilometres'. I asked about the car's features and was told it had 'seats, steering wheel, a bonnet and an exhaust pipe'. Tidy-up time interrupted our conversation that day and I didn't see Brendon again until the Monday of the next week. On that Monday he was again in the block corner building another Ferrari. I had decided that if I was going to get Brendon to incorporate other materials into his play I would probably have most success with drawing and writing materials. I waited until he had completed the basic construction of his car and then asked if he had noticed that a car had writing on it – to tell people what type of car it is. I then asked him if he would like to make a sign for his car to tell the others in the group about it.

There was a great response to such a small suggestion. Brendon agreed that a sign was a very good idea and got paper and felt pens to make one. He thought that it needed to be a 'proper' sign and asked me how to draw the words. He wanted the sign to read 'Ferrari – very fast – 151 kms', exactly as he had told me on the first day. I wrote out the

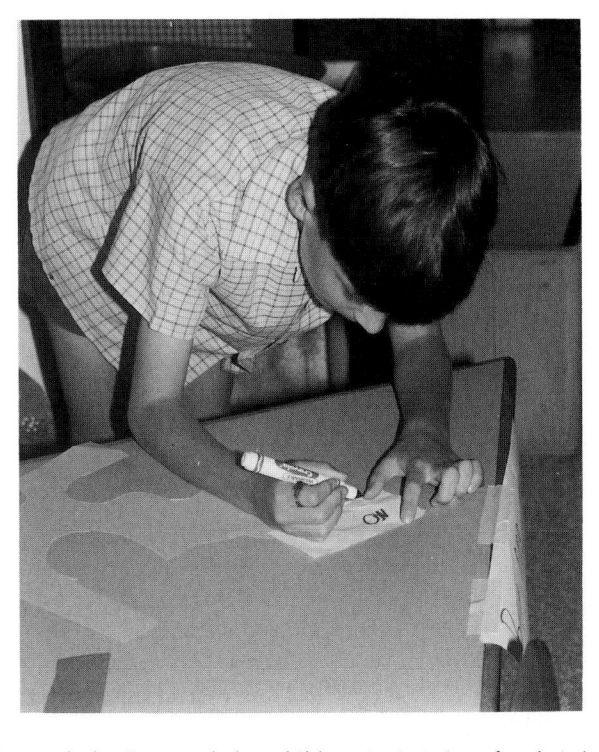

Plate 7.3 Pretend play is extended as children 'write' signs for their buildings and games. (Photo courtesy of Northgate State Preschool.)

words and he copied them. He then proceeded to decorate the sign with some collage materials, and we worked out how the sign could be attached to his car. He and Alyssa, his partner in play, then decided that more signs were necessary and spent much time using the collage and drawing materials making them.

I was thrilled by this enthusiastic response and resolved to try to have some further input. I remembered I had a book about cars at home which showed the parts of cars in simple but informative illustrations. I decided to show this book to Brendon. Due to my illness, however, I did not see Brendon again until my final week and I did not know whether he had continued with his car play. He was at the computer first thing on my first day back, so I decided I would just give him the book. His reply was, 'I'll keep it in mind,' which I didn't think was very promising but again I was surprised by his response. That book became Brendon's 'bible' for the remaining sessions I had with him. It was constantly open and referred to, as Brendon's car was made a motor with cylinders, a battery, brakes, hand brake, accelerator and the like. There were further developments too, such as breakdowns which required tools to fix them, and a flat battery which needed a battery charger which had to be made. Other children, both girls and boys, became involved in the play, either by assisting Brendon or building their own cars which then developed major mechanical problems.

In reflecting on her experience, Lynette wrote:

> I really couldn't have hoped for a better result from a very small amount of intervention. I had not previously engaged in children's play in this way. I have realized that the timing and type of intervention is crucial if it is not to be intrusive. By taking time to observe and casually ask questions I got to know what Brendon knew about cars. Because I felt he was missing out on using other materials, the suggestion about signs seemed a way to broaden his experiences as well as extend his play.
>
> His use of the book, which gave him more detailed information on cars, showed me how valuable the provision of factual information can be to preschool-age children if it is presented in a meaningful context. I wonder about what contributed to the richer play. Was it the new information provided by the book which gave more purpose to the children's play, or was it that my interest made them feel that it was OK to play? Perhaps both factors contributed.

Lynette's reflections on her experience in extending children's play contain many similar comments to those mentioned by other students when reflecting on their experiences. Have you noticed that all students expressed surprise and delight either at the positive effects of their actions and interaction with children or at the knowledge they had gained from seeking to achieve their goals? Many also commented that their experiences had confirmed their beliefs or had convinced them of the value of a particular strategy or teaching approach. For some of the students, too, along with this growing understanding there came more questioning. If you are prepared to reflect on your teaching, you, too, can experience this delight and increased knowledge as well as the challenge of seeking answers to the questions that will inevitably arise. In the process you will become a better teacher.

REFLECTING ON TEACHING

Although, throughout this book, experiences and stories have been related which have highlighted the importance and value of reflection for the person concerned, it is possible that you may still have some questions and wonderings about:

- the nature of reflection;
- how you can reflect effectively;
- why engaging in reflection will be of benefit to you.

By looking more closely at the stories in this chapter in the light of some of the theory about reflection, you may find some answers to your particular questions.

Reflective teaching has become a familiar term in teacher education in recent years (Calderhead, 1989; Richardson, 1990; Zeichner and Liston, 1987), although it is not a new term. Dewey (1909/1933: 9), for instance, highlighted reflection as a means of carefully and persistently considering a belief or form of knowledge 'in the light of the grounds that support it and the further conclusions to which it tends'. Schon (1983, 1987) built on Dewey's notion and talked about *knowledge-in-action* and *reflection-in-action*. Schon's knowledge-in-action concept describes situations where you may use a tacit type of knowledge which you cannot consciously articulate at the time. Reflection-in-action, in contrast, is where you *consciously* interact with a problematic situation. In other words, you are thinking about the problem by drawing on various knowledge sources in order to develop strategies and test out possible solutions. If you think back to the students' goal setting and stories, you can see that they were engaging in reflection-in-action.

Reflecting assists in defining teaching problems and questions

In order to set their personal goals the students first had to reflect on their teaching in ways that led them to define a practical problem or question which they saw as needing some solutions or answers. Kylie, for instance, was keen to discover the extent to which her own values influenced her teaching decisions and children's behaviour, whereas Cindy and Lynette wanted to find answers to their question of how to support children so that they could have more input and control over their own learning. Bronwyn and Susan were concerned to find some practical solutions for building relationships and promoting cooperation, while Monica was concerned with minimizing the problem of aggressive behaviour and helping a child gain more self-control. The more clearly a problem or question can be defined, the more likely it is that meaningful solutions will be found.

Reflecting requires a conscious consideration of the problem

As the students went about finding *their* solution to *their* problem, it was apparent that they had to do more than just apply a technical skill. They had to engage in an active and deliberate consideration of the problem. They did this in a number of ways. First, they described the problem in some detail and considered possible factors that were contributing to it. Then they drew on their own past experiences, the experience and knowledge of others such as their supervising teacher, as well as on specialized knowledge and the suggested strategies they had gained from their readings in order to propose possible ways of overcoming the problem. They also had to consider the

171

particular contexts in which they were working in order to assess whether their proposed actions were appropriate. Then they had to put their proposed solution to the test – *they had to engage in practical action and reflect further on the consequences of that action.*

Reflecting demands detailed description of actions and responses

Did you notice that in telling their stories each student spent some time describing their actions and the responses of others involved – both children and adults? Description is regarded by some teacher educators as a vital aspect of learning to reflect and to teach (Perry, 1995). This stems from the view that teachers store their knowledge of teaching in fairly large chunks or scripts of events. These descriptions are not only seen to help build an awareness of the complexity of classrooms, but also to 'provide the form in which teachers' meanings are stored, conveyed and brought to bear on novel instances in problem solving' (Doyle, 1990: 356). If description is to be used in this way, it is important that your descriptions contain details which show how your actions and reactions are linked to the actions and reactions of others involved. Monica, for instance, highlighted these links in her story, describing how she put some suggested strategies into action and how Jason responded to them. She also described particular features of the environment at particular times of the day that appeared to contribute to or ease Jason's difficulties.

Reflecting involves clarifying reasons for the effects of actions

Another feature of the students' stories was their evaluation relating to their goals. In all the stories the students indicated that they had achieved their goals, at least to some degree. (Remember, though, that your reflections can be just as meaningful in terms of your learnings, even if you do not achieve your goal, provided they help you understand the reasons why.) Did you notice that the students drew on their descriptions of what had happened to clarify reasons why a particular action or strategy had been successful? Rachel's story, for example, gave many brief descriptions of what she did to promote effective organization. Identifying reasons for success, or lack of it, is a key element in learning to teach because, if you can build your knowledge of why and how specific actions affect specific situations, you have a firm base from which to hypothesize, predict and make decisions.

SUMMARY

The experiences shared by these student teachers have highlighted a number of actions that you can take in order to make the most of your teaching practice. First of all, you need to reflect on your past experiences of teaching and the current state of your knowledge with a view to defining some questions about teaching or outlining a particular difficulty or problem you have experienced in your teaching. From this type of thinking you can set yourself some personal goals to achieve during your teaching practice. Next, you have to seek and gather information, and formulate strategies which will assist you to achieve your particular goals. The testing out of your proposed strategies and the evaluation of their effectiveness in your teaching practice setting follows.

Reflection brings an added dimension to your understanding of all your actions. As illustrated in the students' stories, it not only helps you identify goals for your teaching but it also assists you to refine your teaching strategies and increases your self-understanding. At the same time it challenges your thinking. Ensuring that you make detailed descriptions of situations which link actions and responses is an important aspect of reflection, because it provides you with a basis for clarifying reasons for the success or otherwise of your actions. As you think further about your own desire and ability to reflect, you may find it useful to ask yourself these questions:

- *Am I developing skills that will help me reflect more effectively?*
  Do I consider a teaching problem by:

  - undertaking readings and research?
  - seeking views from experienced others?
  - analysing situational influences?
  - testing out some strategies in practice and observing effects and responses?
  - describing these actions and their effects in sufficient detail so they can be further reflected upon?
  - assessing the consequences of actions in the light of my knowledge and beliefs?

- *What am I gaining from reflecting?*
  Am I able to use the knowledge and insight gained to:

  - clarify and give reasons for my actions?
  - make teaching decisions that are based on a sound rationale?
  - help me better understand my own teaching decisions and actions?
  - raise questions and issues that challenge my current thinking?
  - consider teaching decisions in the light of moral and ethical perspectives?

CONCLUSION

As you consider your answers to these questions about reflection, you will simultaneously be considering your answers to questions about teaching, too, because the ability to reflect is inherent in the ability to teach. How you respond to these questions is up to you. Your response, however, is not a matter that can be taken lightly. This is because teaching requires you to make 'concrete choices among competing values for vulnerable others who lack the teacher's knowledge and skills ... and who will be changed by what the teacher teaches, how it is taught and who that teacher is' (Cuban, 1992: 9).

This book has been written in the hope that you will develop your understanding of teaching to the point where you can make wise choices. While it has highlighted some of the factors and influences that will guide your decisions about 'what' and 'how' to teach, it has emphasised that ultimately you will have to take responsibility for some complex decision making in this regard. The question of 'who' the teacher should be has also been addressed – although perhaps more indirectly – by indicating the kinds of modelling a teacher needs to provide and the types of messages a teacher needs to convey if children are to be confident, constructive and cooperative learners. Again, however, you are the only one who can decide 'who' you are as a teacher.

SUGGESTED ACTIVITIES

- In small groups discuss one student's story that was presented in this chapter, and consider features of the way in which that student went about achieving the goal that had been set. Would you have approached it in a similar or different way? Outline some reasons for your response.

- Prior to your next teaching practice, or at the conclusion of a period of teaching practice, engage in some personal goal setting using the steps outlined in this chapter. You may want to select an area of your teaching in which you feel reasonably confident because you want to refine your skills further. Alternatively, you may want to set goals in an area which is problematic or in which you feel inadequate. Outline the reasons for the selection of your goal.

- Write a reflective story which details your experiences in seeking to achieve a personal goal relating to teaching. Provide details of:
  - how and why the strategies designed to achieve the goal were developed and used;
  - how you evaluated whether or not you had achieved your goal;
  - what you have learned and what else you would like to know or are wondering about.

- Look back over journal entries, programme folders, or observation and planning records you have made during previous teaching practice experiences. Examine them critically to see if there is evidence of some of the processes seen to be essential for effective reflection. After this consideration write down some actions you could take which would improve your ability to reflect. Decide how you will record your reflections during teaching practice.

- In small groups discuss whether or not you agree with the statement by Cuban (1992: 9) '[children] will be changed by what the teacher teaches, how it is taught and who that teacher is'. If you agree with the statement, write down some of the factors and influences that will guide your decisions about 'what' and 'how' to teach. Think about some of the things you do when you are with children. What picture do you think children are building of you as a person? What qualities would you hope they would perceive you to have as their teacher?

REFERENCES

Allen, K.E. and Marotz, L. (1989) *Developmental Profiles: Birth to Six*, New York: Delmar Publishing.

Almy, M. and Genishi, C. (1979) *Ways of Studying Children*, New York: Teachers College Press.

Anning, A. (ed.) (1995) *A National Curriculum for the Early Years*, Buckingham: Open University Press.

Aubrey, C. (ed.) (1994) *The Role of Subject Knowledge in the Early Years of Schooling*, London: Falmer Press.

Beaty, J. (1990) *Observing Development of the Young Child*, New York: Macmillan.

Berger, K.S. (1991) *The Developing Person through Childhood and Adolescence*, New York: Worth Publishers.

Berk, L.E. (1994) *Infants and Children: Prenatal through Middle Childhood*, Needham, MA: Allyn & Bacon.

Berk, L.E. and Winsler, A. (1995) *Scaffolding Children's Learning: Vygotsky and Early Childhood Education*, Washington, DC: National Association for the Education of Young Children.

Blenkin, G.V. and Kelly, A.V. (eds) (1988) *Early Childhood Education: A Developmental Curriculum*, London: Paul Chapman.

—— (eds) (1992) *Assessment in Early Childhood Education*, London: Paul Chapman.

—— (eds) (1994) *A National Curriculum and Early Learning: An Evaluation*, London: Paul Chapman.

Bredekamp, S. (ed.) (1987) *Developmentally Appropriate Practice in Early Childhood Programs Serving Children from Birth through Age 8*, Washington, DC: National Association for the Education of Young Children.

—— (1991) 'Guidelines for appropriate curriculum content and assessment in programs serving children ages three through eight', *Young Children*, 46 (3): 21–38.

Bredekamp, S. and Rosegrant, T. (eds) (1992) *Reaching Potentials: Appropriate Curriculum and Assessment for Young Children*, vol. 1, Washington, DC: National Association for the Education of Young Children.

—— (eds) (1995) *Reaching Potentials: Transforming Early Childhood Curriculum and Assessment*, vol. 2, Washington, DC: National Association for the Education of Young Children.

Bronson, M.B. (1995) *The Right Stuff for Children Birth to 8: Selecting Play Materials to Support Development*, Washington, DC: National Association for the Education of Young Children.

Bruner, J. (1986) *Actual Minds – Possible Worlds*, London: Harvard University Press.

Caine, R.N. and Caine, G. (1990) 'Understanding a brain-based approach to learning and teaching', *Educational Leadership*, 48 (2): 66–70.

REFERENCES

Calderhead, J. (1989) 'Reflective teaching and teacher education', *Teaching and Teacher Education* 5: 43–51.

Cohen, L. and Manion, L. (1993) *A Guide to Teaching Practice*, London: Routledge.

Connelly, F.M. and Clandinin, D.J. (1988) *Teachers as Curriculum Planners: Narratives of Experience*, New York: Teachers College Press.

Cox, T. and Sanders, S. (1994) *The Impact of the National Curriculum on the Teaching of Five Year Olds*, London: Falmer Press.

Creaser, B. and Dau, E. (1996) *The Anti-bias Approach in Early Childhood*, Sydney: HarperCollins.

Crittenden, B. (1996) *Thinking about Education: Essays for Discussion in Teacher Education*, Melbourne: Addison Wesley Longman.

Cross, T. (1995) 'The early childhood curriculum debate', in M. Fleer (ed.) *DAPcentrism: Challenging Developmentally Appropriate Practice*, Watson, ACT: Australian Early Childhood Association.

Cuban, L. (1992) 'Managing dilemmas while building professional communities', *Educational Researcher*, 21 (1): 4–11.

Derman-Sparks, L. and the ABC Task Force (1989) *Anti-bias Curriculum: Tools for Empowering Young Children*, Washington, DC: National Association for the Education of Young Children.

DeVries, R. and Kohlberg, L. (1990) *Constructivist Early Education: Overview and Comparison with Other Programs*, Washington, DC: National Association for the Education of Young Children.

Dewey, J. (1933) *How We Think*, Boston: Heath (First published 1909).

Doyle, W. (1990) 'Classroom knowledge as a foundation for teaching', *Teachers College Record*, 91 (3): 347–60.

Ebbeck, M.A. (1991) *Early Childhood Education*, Melbourne: Longman Cheshire.

Edwards, A. and Knight, P. (1994) *Effective Early Years Education: Teaching Young Children*, Buckingham: Open University Press.

Eisner, E. (1985) *The Educational Imagination: On the Design and Evaluation of School Programs*, New York: Macmillan.

Elkind, D. (1989) 'Developmentally appropriate practice: philosophical and practical implications', *Phi Delta Kappan* (October): 113–17.

Fisher, J. (1993) 'A descriptive analysis of the development of reflective practice in an early years classroom', paper presented at the European Conference on the Quality of Early Childhood Education (3rd), Reading, England, EDRS Document ED 366414 PS 021 826.

Fortson, L.R. and Reiff, J. (1995) *Early Childhood Curriculum: Open Structures for Integrative Learning*, Needham Heights, MA: Allyn & Bacon.

Genishi, C. (ed.) (1992) *Ways of Assessing Children and Curriculum: Stories of Early Childhood Practice*, New York: Teachers College Press.

Gordon, T. (1974) *TET: Teacher Effectiveness Training*, New York: Peter H. Wyden.

Greenman, J. (1988) *Caring Spaces, Learning Places: Children's Environments that Work*, Redmond, WA: Exchange Press.

'Guidelines for ethical practice in early childhood field experience', (1995) The Early Childhood Practicum Council of NSW.

'Guidelines for preparation of early childhood professionals', (1996) Washington, DC: National Association for the Education of Young Children.

Handal, G. and Lauvås, P. (1987) *Promoting Reflective Teaching: Supervision in Action*, Milton Keynes: Open University Press.

Harper, J. and Richards, L. (1986) *Mothers and Working Mothers*, Melbourne: Pelican Books.

Hatch, J.A. (1988) 'Kindergarten philosophies and practices: perspectives of teachers, principals, and supervisors', *Early Childhood Research Quarterly*, 3: 151–66.

REFERENCES

Hendrick, J. (1990) *Total Learning: Developmental Curriculum for the Young Child*, New York: Macmillan.

Henry, M. (1996) *Young Children, Parents and Professionals*, London: Routledge.

Hobart, L., Self, K. and Ward, J. (1994) 'Beginning teachers exploring their own knowledge', in *Knowledge and Competence for Beginning Teachers*, Brisbane: Queensland Board of Teacher Registration.

Honig, A. (1993) 'Outcomes of infant and toddler care', *Montessori Life* (Fall): 34–42.

Katz, L. (1984) 'The professional early childhood teacher', *Young Children* (July): 3–10.

—— (1987) 'The nature of professions: where is early childhood education?' *Current Topics in Early Childhood Education*, vol. 7, Norwood, NJ: Ablex.

—— (1995a) 'The professional preschool teacher', in L.G. Katz (ed.) *Talks with Teachers of Young Children: A Collection*, Norwood, NJ: Ablex.

—— (1995b) 'Ethical issues in working with young children', in L.G. Katz (ed.) *Talks with Teachers of Young Children: A Collection*, Norwood, NJ: Ablex.

—— (1996) 'Children as learners: a developmental approach', *Conference Proceedings*, Weaving Webs Conference: Collaborative Teaching and Learning in the Early Years Curriculum, University of Melbourne (July): 133–46.

Katz, L. and Chard, S. (1989) *Engaging Children's Minds: The Project Approach*, Norwood, NJ: Ablex.

Kostelnik, M. J., Soderman, A. and Whiren, A. (1993) *Developmentally Appropriate Programs in Early Childhood Education*, New York: Macmillan.

Lambert, B. (1992) 'Field experience in early childhood tertiary courses: making or breaking a professional image', in B. Lambert (ed.) *Changing Faces: The Early Childhood Profession in Australia*, Watson, ACT: Australian Early Childhood Association.

Leach, P. (1994) *Children First*, Harmondsworth: Penguin.

Løvlie, L. (1974) Pedagogisk filosofi for praktiserende laerere (Philosophy of education for practising teachers), *Pedagogen*, 1 (22): 19–36, cited in G. Handal, and P. Lauvås, (1987) *Promoting Reflective Teaching: Supervision in Action*, Milton Keynes: Open University Press.

McAfee, O. and Leong, D. (1994) *Assessing and Guiding Young Children's Development and Learning*, Needham Heights, MA: Allyn & Bacon.

MacNaughton, G. and Clyde, M. (1990) 'Staffing the practicum: towards a new set of basics through clarifying roles', Paper presented at the National Workshop on Early Childhood Practicum (1st), Frankston, Victoria (June), EDRS Document ED 338365 PS019826.

Meade-Roberts, J., Jones, E. and Hillard, J. (1993) 'Change making in a primary school: Saedad, California', in E. Jones (ed.) *Growing Teachers: Partnerships in Staff Development*, Washington, DC: National Association for the Education of Young Children.

Mindes, G., Ireton, H. and Mardell-Czudnowski, C. (1996) *Assessing Young Children*, Albany, NY: Delmar Publishers.

Moyles, J.R. (1992) *Organizing for Learning in the Primary Classroom: A Balanced Approach to Classroom Management*, Buckingham: Open University Press.

Nicolson, S. and Shipstead, S. (1994) *Through the Looking Glass: Observations in the Early Childhood Classroom*, New York: Macmillan.

Perry, R. (1988) 'An examination of two contrasting approaches to teaching preschool children and their effects on linguistic and social behaviour', unpublished PhD thesis, Brisbane: University of Queensland.

—— (1989) 'What makes Tim – Tim? Some teachers thoughts on observation', unpublished report of preschool director's working party, Brisbane: Queensland Department of Education.

REFERENCES

—— (1995) 'The role of description in reflective teaching', *Journal of Australian Research in Early Childhood Education*, 1: 111–20.

Phyfe-Perkins, E. (1980) 'Children's behaviour in preschool settings: a review of research concerning the influence of the physical environment', in L.G. Katz, C.H. Watkins, M.Quest and M. Spencer (eds) *Current Topics in Early Childhood Education*, vol. 3, Norwood, NJ: Ablex.

Phyfe-Perkins, E., and Shoemaker, J. (1986) 'Indoor play environments: research and design implications,' in G. Fein and M. Rivkin (eds) *The Young Child at Play: Reviews of Research*, vol. 4, Washington, DC: National Association for the Education of Young Children.

Piaget, J. (1964) Quoted in R.E. Ripple and V.E. Rockcastle (eds) *Piaget Rediscovered: A Report of the Conference on Cognitive Studies and Curriculum Development*, Ithaca, NY: School of Education, Cornell University, cited in D. Elkind, (1989) 'Developmentally appropriate practice: philosophical and practical implications,' *Phi Delta Kappan* (October): 113–17.

Posner, George (1993) *Field Experience: A Guide to Reflective Teaching*, New York: Longman.

Rathus, S.A. (1988) *Understanding Child Development*, New York: Holt, Rinehart & Winston.

Richardson, V. (1990) 'The evolution of reflective teaching and teacher education', in R. Clift, W.Houston and M. Pugach (eds) *Encouraging Reflective Practice in Education*, New York: Teachers College Press.

Rodd, J. (1994) *Leadership in Early Childhood: The Pathway to Professionalism*, St Leonards, NSW: Allen & Unwin.

Rubin, K., Fein, G. and Vandenberg, B. (1983) 'Play', in E.M. Hetherington (ed.) *Socialization, Personality and Social Development, vol. 4, Handbook of Child Psychology*, New York: John Wiley.

Schon, D. (1983) *The Reflective Practitioner*, New York: Basic Books.

—— (1987) *Educating the Reflective Practitioner*, San Francisco: Jossey-Bass.

School Curriculum and Assessment Authority (1995) *Nursery Education: Desirable Outcomes for Children's Learning on Entering Compulsory Schooling*, London: SCAA.

Sebastian-Nickell, P. and Milne, R. (1992) *Care and Education of Young Children*, Melbourne: Longman Cheshire.

Shepard, L.A. and Smith, M.A. (1986) 'Synthesis of research on school readiness and kindergarten retention', *Educational Leadership*, 44, (3): 78–86.

Smith, D.L. and Lovat, T.J. (1991) *Curriculum: Action on Reflection*, Wentworth Falls, NSW: Social Science Press.

Smith, P.K. and Connolly, K.J. (1980) *The Ecology of Preschool Behaviour*, Cambridge: Cambridge University Press.

Spodek, B. (1988) 'The implicit theories of early childood teachers', *Early Child Development and Care*, 38: 13 –32.

—— (1991) 'Reconceptualizing early childhood education', *Early Education and Development*, 2 (2): 161 –7.

—— (1993) 'Curriculum alternatives in early childhood education: a historical perspective', in B. Spodek (ed.) *Handbook of Research on the Education of Young Children*, New York: Macmillan.

Sroufe, L.A. (1985) 'Attachment classification from the perspective of infant-caregiver relationships and infant temperament', *Child Development*, 56: 1–4.

Sroufe, L.A., Cooper, R.G. and De Hart, G.B. (1992) *Child Development: Its Nature and Course*, 2nd edn, New York: McGraw-Hill.

Stacey, M. (1991) *Parents and Teachers Together: Partnership in Primary and Nursery Education*, Buckingham: Open University Press.

REFERENCES

Stonehouse, A. (ed.) (1988) *Trusting Toddlers: Programming for One to Three Year Olds in Child Care Centres*, Fyshwick, ACT: Australian Early Childhood Association.

Thomas, S. (1985) *The Diary of a Preschool Teacher*, Brisbane: Queensland Department of Education.

Tisher, R.D. (1987) 'Australian research on the practicum during the last decade', in P. Hughes (ed.) *Better Teachers for Better Schools*, Australian College of Education, Victoria.

Toffler, A. (1974) *Learning for Tomorrow: The Role of the Future in Education*, New York: Vintage.

Walsh, P. (1988) *Early Childhood Playgrounds: Planning an Outside Learning Environment*, Albert Park, Victoria: Robert Anderson & Associates.

Wortham, S.C. (1994) *Early Childhood Curriculum: Developmental Bases for Learning and Teaching*, New York: Macmillan.

Zeichner, K.M. and Liston, D.P. (1987) 'Teaching student teachers to reflect,' *Harvard Educational Review*, 57 (1): 23–48.

INDEX